"One of the most important boo

ASTONISHINGLY IN ..."

—Rolling Stone

*"**Dr. Dre changed things when he did The Chronic** and took something like Leon Haywood's 'I Want' a Do Something Freaky to You' and revamped it in his own way but basically kept the rhythm and instrumental hook intact. It's easier to sample a groove than it is to create a whole new collage. That entire collage element is out the window."*

—Chuck D

"The Chronic set a standard for production that has never been exceeded!"

—The Source

*"**He's changed the culture with his music...** The hardest thing in the world for anybody as driven and talented as Dre is to be successful both personally and professionally... That's what he's striving for, and I believe he's succeeding. He's striking that balance. I have an enormous amount of respect for him."*

—Jimmy Iovine, Interscope C.E.O. and longtime Dr. Dre business partner and Aftermath Entertainment Distributor

*"Eminem crashed the mainstream in the late 90's, creating a storm of controversy and recordbreaking sales not seen since Snoop Dogg's debut. **With super-producer Dr. Dre behind the boards, Eminem scored mega-hits.**" —Rolling Stone*

*"Dre feels like **God placed him here to make music**, and no matter what forces are aligned against him, **he always ends up on the mountaintop.**"*

—Kanye West

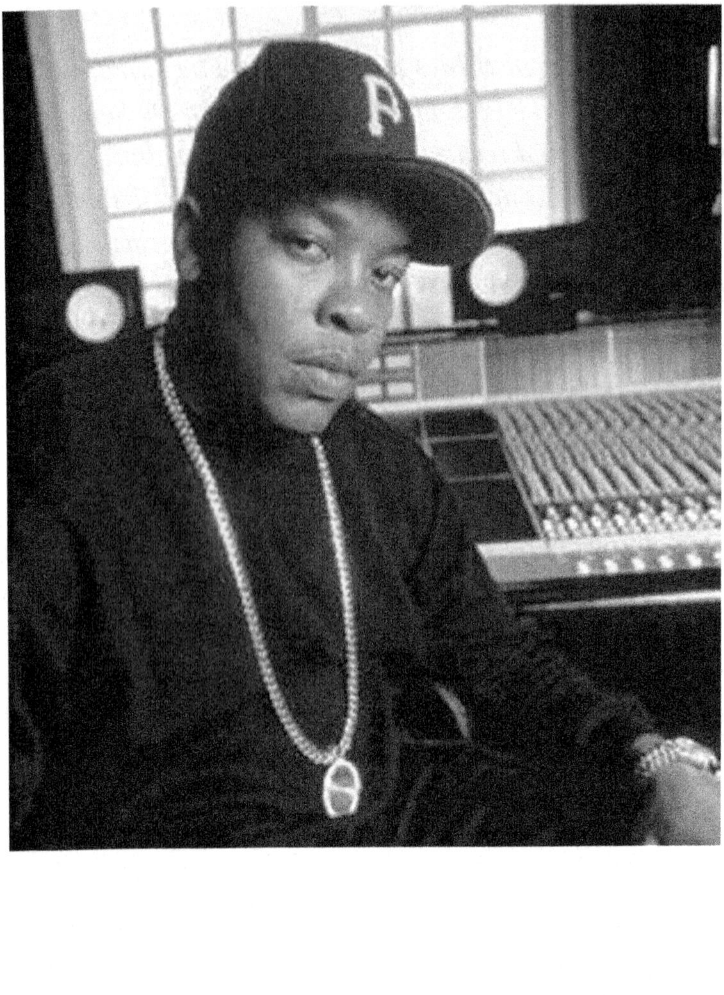

DR. DRE IN THE STUDIO:

From Compton, Death Row, Snoop Dogg, Eminem,
50 Cent, The Game and Mad Money
The Life, Times and Aftermath of
the Notorious Record Producer—DR. DRE

by Jake Brown

Colossus Books
Phoenix
New York   Los Angeles

DR. DRE IN THE STUDIO:
From Compton, Death Row, Snoop Dogg, Eminem,
0 Cent, The Game and Mad Money —The Life, Times and Aftermath of
the Notorious Record Producer—DR. DRE

By Jake Brown

Published by:
Colossus Books
A Division of Amber Communications Group, Inc.
1334 East Chandler Boulevard, Suite 5-D67
Phoenix, AZ 85048
Amberbk@aol.com
WWW.AMBERBOOKS.COM

Tony Rose, Publisher/Editorial Director
Samuel P. Peabody, Associate Publisher
Yvonne Rose, Associate Publisher/Senior Editor
The Printed Page, Interior Design/Cover Layout

ALL RIGHTS RESERVED

No part of this book may be reproduced or transmitted in any form or by any means – electronic or mechanical, including photocopying, recording or by any information storage and retrieved system without written permission from the authors, except for the inclusion of brief quotations in a review.

The publication is designed to provide accurate and authoritative information in regard to the subject matter covered. It is sold with the understanding that the Publisher is not engaged in rendering legal, accounting or other professional services. If legal advice or other expert assistance is required, the services of a competent professional person should be sought.

COLOSSUS BOOKS are available at special discounts for bulk purchases, sales promotions, fund raising or educational purposes.

© Copyright 2006 by Jake Brown & Amber Books
ISBN#: 0-9767735-5-4 / 978-0-9767735-5-9
Library of Congress Control Number: 200693456

Contents

Introduction	1
Chapter 1 – The DJ Dr. Dre…	3
Chapter 2 – World Class Wrecking Crew	9
Chapter 3 – N.W.A. is Born	13
Chapter 4 – No One Can Do it Better – Dr. Dre & D.O.C.	23
Chapter 5 – The Chronic	37
Chapter 6 – Doggystyle	45
Chapter 7 – The Aftermath of G-Funk is Born…	53
Chapter 8 – 1997-1999	61
Photos	67
Chapter 9 – Eminem	73
Chapter 10 – The Chronic 2001	85
Chapter 11 – 2000-2001	97
Chapter 12 – 50 Cent	105
Chapter 13 – 2002-2005	121
Conclusion	132
Dr. Dre Solo Discography (Partial)…	141
About the Author	153

Dr. Dre in the Studio

Dedication

*Dedicated to my dear friend Penelope Ellis
for keeping your head up...*

Dr. Dre in the Studio

"Irrefutably one of the most important artists in the history of hip-hop, if not all popular music, Dr. Dre has amassed an astonishingly impressive body of work over his lengthy career."

—*Rolling Stone Magazine*

Introduction

Looking out upon Dr. Dre's legacy is like looking up at a galaxy, or arguably a Universe, where there aren't just single stars he's made, but constellations of stars spanning the multiple generations and worlds beyond what anyone else could have envisioned for hip hop's sound and evolution over the past 25 years. Dr. Dre's beats alone are futuristic enough to be comparable to the outer space metaphor, in that they take us to a new frontier of advancement in both musical soundscapes and sophistication of the science of beat-making with every new album or single he produces. Each new hit is an exercise in creative time travel, pushing past the known boundaries of whatever is considered most cutting edge at the time of its commercial release.

Moreover, one can listen back 15 years to 1989 when the D.O.C.'s 'No One Can Do It Better' was released and clearly hear that the album was ahead of its time from a production vantage point. The same was true of the landmark 'Chronic' album three years later, which spawned hip hop's greatest single revolution in terms of musical and commercial blending and branding with the G-Funk era. Often as quiet as the nighttime sky about the secrets to his craft, perhaps Dr. Dre in his own head speaks a language too advanced for us to understand. Perhaps it resembles something like the Matrix, but sounds like the musical version of the Oracle.

As a producer, Dr. Dre is certainly prophetic, so the analogy can't be that off base, even if you disagree with the chosen likening. Much like a medic in a chaotic situation, the industry looks to Dr. Dre for guidance. Whenever hip hop finds itself in critical commercial condition and in need of a stylistic transplant, Dr. Dre performs under pressure, and delivers every time. His beats have been literal miracles for a genre that could have been stunted permanently in evolution countless times had it not been for N.W.A. in 1987, or the D.O.C. in 1989, or the Chronic in 1992, or Snoop Dogg in 1994, or Eminem in 1998, or 50 Cent in 2002, and on and on in to the present place in the millennium, where again we wait on Dr. Dre's third solo album, 'Detox.'

In the interim, through the pages of 'Dr. Dre in the Studio' we can look back as students at the professor's catalog and consider this examination only the cliff notes. It will take generations to fully understand the depth of Dr. Dre's science as a producer and the impact of his musical advancements, both in their moment and for the future…

"I would definitely not be as good of a producer if I hadn't started DJing. Because that's where I really started paying attention to how records are made. I would critique and just listen and say, 'I would have done this different.' So that definitely was a stepping-stone to what I'm doing now...."

—*Dre*

Chapter 1
The D.J. Dr. Dre...

Any of the greatest musical genres spanning throughout the sonic ages—regardless of which medium they fell in, i.e. blues rock in the case of Jimmy Hendrix; funk alt-pop in the case of Prince; grunge in the case of Kurt Cobain; hard rock in the case of the Rolling Stones; heavy metal in the case of Led Zepplin; or G-Funk hip hop in the case of Dr. Dre—all came in a time when they weren't expected but were desperately needed.

No matter how little one style might have had socially or stylistically to do with another, what graduated them all from the same school was their originality, as well as the lack of comparative likeness to anything else going on around them. Each spawned an infectious and culturally lasting scene and style of its own based foundationally on the vibe the musical first gave off to its listeners. For instance, in the case of Jimmy Hendrix, though his living legend lasted only 4 short years, the musical ground he covered in that time would span generations after his death.

Tupac Shakur had much the same effect on hip hop from a lyrical point of view, but only one other musical presence in rap has been as equally dominant or forceful in shaping the direction of the genre. That entity comes in the form of producer/rapper Dr. Dre.

Pioneer would be too shortsighted a way to look at the groundwork he has laid in his 25 years in the game. One would have to be looking down upon his soundscape from the overarching angle of the (entire world of music) he shaped through his sound—much as you might look at a globe of the earth. Spinning hip hop's, you'd find different landscapes, different cultures, different demographics of people standing for different things, messages, ideologies and territories that conflicted with one another, and so forth.

One singular thing keeps the gravity of this world intact, and that is the music that lays beneath the lyrical foundations that often times provoke conflict and differences to flair up within the world of hip hop. Whether it's Public Enemy rapping about political oppression, or Nelly rapping about good times, music has always shaped the message. Statistically, its been proven time and again that hip hop listeners listen to the beat before anything else in determining if they groove to a song.

It's an indiscriminate passion that first drives any music listener, whereafter they graduate to a lyrical appreciation that elevates their enjoyment to a whole other level. But it always, always begins with the music. As Dr. Dre himself qualified the latter, "coming from a DJ background, I knew as a producer that if the song don't grab your ear in the first 30 seconds, you're going to change the station."

Chapter 1. The D.J. Dr. Dre...

Not surprisingly, Dre began training to become an entertainer "back when I was like 3 and 4 years old, I would play records for my mother's card parties. I'd put a record on and people would scream out or get up and dance. I just loved stirring people up." Elaborating on the ready and regular presence of music in his household growing up, Dre recalls that "I can remember when I was just like about 4 years old in Compton...and my mother would have me stack 45s, stack about 10 of them, and when one would finish, the next record would drop. Do you remember those old record players that played 45s? It was like I was DJ'ing for the house, picking out certain songs and stacking them so this song would go after that song.

I would go to sleep with headphones on, listening to music. My mom and my pop—they would have music so loud, loud enough to shake the walls...I think music was my mom's release from the pressures of working two jobs and all...When she got home at night, the stereo came on even before the lights." Growing up during the 1970s to the sounds of Curtis Mayfield, Barry White, Isaac Hayes, and of course, George Clinton, Dre explained that "I'm a big P-Funk fan, that was it for me growing up. Curtis Mayfield, Isaac Hayes, I was influenced by all of those guys. That's what really motivated me to use live instruments on my records. Just listening to the way they put their records together. That appreciation came from my mother. There was always music being played in my house when I was growing up, and that's all I heard was 70's soul. And then the DJing thing came along."

Beginning his career in the game as a DJ—at Compton block parties of all places—Dr. Dre faced the pressure of having drinks thrown at him if the crowd didn't like his mix of popular hits at the time—and there was no chicken wire to protect him from an unhappy audience. That sort of gun-to-his-head intensity (not quite literally, but given the neighborhood, not that far from reality in context) worked to hone Dre's ability to keep his aural finger on the pulse of what kind of sound was required to satisfy his listening audience in the moment, i.e. to craft a sound that was instantly current.

From this foundation, Dre could then innovate his mixes to offer the audience something new, explaining that "I DJ'ed at (the Los Angeles dance club) Eve After Dark, I would put together this mix shelf, lots of oldies, Martha and the Vandellas and stuff like that, and where normally you go to a club and the DJs play all the hit records back to back, I used to put on a serious show. People would come from everywhere just to see Dr. Dre on the wheels of steel…A little later, I used to take Ice Cube up to Skateland in Compton—he was in a group with my cousin at the time—and I would tell him that with this crowd you'd better get up and rock, because if you didn't, they'd throw these full cups at your ass. I would have Cube and my cousin change the words to certain songs—like 'My Adidas' became 'My Penis'—and the crowd would get going, and I'd be mixing. That was the dope."

In essence, Dre was learning to create trends by taking a classic sample and reinventing it with his own spin of the record.

Chapter 1. The D.J. Dr. Dre...

Discussing the roots of his desire to DJ, even prior to producing, Dre credits "Grandmaster Flash (with)...motivating me to want to DJ...I heard 'The Adventures of Grandmaster Flash on the Wheels of Steel' and I was blown away. So, me and a friend of mine at the time decided to tear apart a couple of component sets and make our own little mixer and two turntables. And not too long after that, my mom got me a mixer, and that was it for me. But I would have to give credit to Grandmaster Flash for getting me into the business."

Using DJing as a stepping stone, Dr. Dre explains the process by which one was a catalyst for the other, such that "I would definitely not be as good of a producer if I hadn't started DJing. Because that's where I really started paying attention to how records are made. I would critique and just listen and say, 'I would have done this different.' So that definitely was a stepping-stone to what I'm doing now...This club I was DJing at, at the time, had a little demo studio in the back of it. I made a couple of demos, played them in the club, and got a good response. So I just started making it a little bit better here and there, and the next thing you know I had a record out. Everybody was digging it, so I decided that this was the job I was going to take."

Continuing, Dre explains that "I would just come in there during the week and just try to create my songs, just messing around, seeing if I had it. I would play them in the clubs on the weekend and I would get good responses, so I just kept doing it and it became my profession.' He continues, 'I learned how to engineer basically from that club. I also learned a lot from this engineer, Donovan, at Audio Achievements in Torrance. We used to work together a lot, and I eventually started working by myself on mixes. I wanted it to sound a certain way and I felt nobody was going to be able to dig in my brain and get the sound out that I wanted except me. Everyday I would learn something new."

Dr. Dre in the Studio

"Dangerous though their lyrics were, Dre's production was equally important to the success of the group. His knack for unforgettable beats, funky bass lines and cinematic depth proved the perfect accompaniment to their confrontational rhymes."

—*Rolling Stone Magazine*

Chapter 2
World Class Wrecking Crew

The genesis of the 'World Class Wrecking Crew' was that of Dr. Dre's own evolution and transition from DJ to producer, giving him his first commercially released album and taste of success with 'Surgery', the modestly successful club hit the group's only album of the same title produced in 1985.

Explaining the process by which W.C.W.C. first gained notice outside of the clubs in South Central Los Angeles, the L.A. Weekly explained that "Don MacMillan, the owner of Macola Records, distributed Wreckin' Cru recordings to an informal network of independent distributors around the country…After modest success with its first 12-inch single, the Cru had a hit with 'Surgery,' a 1984 number written and produced by Dre that sold 50,000 records—a huge amount for an independently made and distributed record. 'Surgery' was typical of the Wreckin' Cru's music: basic electronic funk, a fast drum machine beat, lots of turntable scratching and silly lyrics ('Calling Dr. Dre to surgery')…The Wreckin' Cru started making the transition from dance hall DJs to recording artists. They followed 'Surgery' with 'Juice' in 1985 and put out an album called 'World Class' that same year. CBS Records called...(Next), and the Wreckin' Cru went on tour as an opening act for Rick James...(While on the road), CBS (called) offering a contract with a $100,000 advance... Dre complained that Lonzo wasn't paying him enough...As much as Dre complained about money, he told friends that he was equally frustrated with the Wreckin' Cru's musical direction."

For Dre, the experience was very much a foot in the door, and a reflection visually of how lost rap was at the time. In later years, at the height of the beef between Dr. Dre and Eazy E, promotional photos would be released displaying Dr. Dre wearing lip stick, something unfortunately common to the times, or he would NEVER have done so.

In contrast to N.W.A.'s hardcore gangsta image, more accurately reflective of the surroundings Dr. Dre had come up in, World Class Wrecking Crew was the equivalent of any plethora of straight-to-video, D-rate movies that any countless number of A-List actors and actresses did in the beginning of their careers for a foot in the door.

As DJ Yella, Dr. Dre's later partner in N.W.A. recalled, W.C.W.C. as a means to an end, "I used to DJ in a club in LA as a teenager. Then Dre came along and we hit it off from the beginning. We deejayed together for years before we even got into the music industry. Hip Hop was like Grandmaster Flash back then. Rap was something from the east coast. We

Chapter 2. World Class Wrecking Crew

almost originally started west coast Hip Hop when we were in the World Class Wrecking Cru. We were broke but we stuck together. We'd seen a show with Run DMC for the first time. It was their first time in California. We sat back and looked at the show and it wasn't nothin'! It was two people rapping and a DJ! We said, 'That's it! We can do that!' That's when we started trying to make records. That's when we put out Surgery. It did okay and we sold a few but me and Dre were getting tired of the Wrecking Cru cuz the money situation wasn't right and we were always broke. We weren't getting paid. So we were looking for a way out. And Dre already knew Eazy. So we waited for the right time and left the Wrecking Crew to start NWA in '86. Originally, there was six of us in NWA—me, MC Ren, Ice Cube, Dr. Dre, Eazy-E and Arabian Prince. But Prince was around for only the first couple of songs; he was just doing his own stuff, I guess. He dropped out a little after we took the picture for the 'Straight Outta Compton' album…Ren was one of the best rappers in NWA, on account of his strong voice. He wasn't a producer, though. Cube was just a writer; he just happened to write some of Eazy's first few songs."

Dre's paring with Eazy E would produce N.W.A. and make history, but prior thereto, within the context of World Class Wrecking Crew as it relates to Dr. Dre's development as a producer, former peer the Arabian Price sheds light on how Dre's time as part of the DJ group helped to prepare him to walk in and fill the shoes that N.W.A. would require of him.

Recalling that "we all was DJs back in the hood, in Compton from different crews and stuff. And me and Dre and Yella used to hang out a lot DJing and working on beats and stuff. Dre was with Yella, and we decided we needed to start this new group, so from there once we hooked up with Eazy, we came up with N.W.A. (Prior to that, when we were producing our sound), we came across Kraftwerk first, and it was always going back and taking 'Trance…Express' and speeding it up, and playing it with some other tracks…(From an image point of view), there weren't that many clubs in the hood, so you had to venture out to go to a lot of clubs, and a lot of the clubs were playing (new wave, so we were naturally influenced by that scene a little bit)."

Continuing, Arabian Prince explains that "out (in LA), even though there was breakin', and that kind of stuff, there was really a lot of freakin' going on in the clubs, the clubs was just nasty back in the early 80s. The Struttin and the Robot was big out (in LA) as well, so a lot of that stuff kind of influenced the Electro movement, and BPMs and stuff like that. With everything back then, nothing was under 125 BPM…We were playing a lot of the (New Wave) stuff because it was the same BMP as the Electro music, so we were mixing that with Electro, and it just kind of fit in. Then slowly but surely that stuff kind of fazed out, and Electro took over, and I often say N.W.A. killed Electro because we did 'Panic Zone' and kind of went 'Okay, we street now 100%.' (In N.W.A.), we all played our own (instruments), because back then I don't even remember having a sampler. My first sampler was an Emulator 2, and that sucker was huge, and even when we moved into N.W.A., even N.W.A. didn't sample. We'd bring in guitar players and bass players. If you listen to that N.W.A. stuff, 75% of it is live music. We had an in-house guitar player we'd bring in, and we'd do the beats on an MP or the SB12, or SB1200, and just rock it like that."

Comically enough, the start of Dr. Dre's affiliation out of World Class Wrecking Crew began with Eazy E began when W.C.W.C.'s manager Lonzo refused to bail Dre out of jail over unpaid parking tickets. As the L.A. Weekly explained, "Eazy and Dre cut a deal: Eazy would bail Dre out of jail; Dre would produce records for Eazy's new record company."

> "In almost any other medium, (N.W.A.'s album) content would have been received more calmly. It would have been analyzed as an artistic stance, not a lifestyle…Dre would have been exalted as a postmodern master, Frank Gehry at the mixing board, cobbling scraps of James Brown funk to cool Euro techno in a way that made both seem more alive."
>
> —*L.A. Weekly*

Chapter 3
N.W.A. Is Born

Being that the Arabian Prince, according to Eazy E, originally wanted to call N.W.A.'s landmark album 'Straight Outta Compton' 'From Compton with Love', it's not rocket science to figure out why the group made more sense with his exit. Leaving Dr. Dre and Yella to assume complete production responsibilities, the group's sound honed itself entirely around a soundscape reflective of the realities of the gang-infested, violence-driven urban battlefield they'd grown up in.

Giving a soundtrack and voice to a reality whose existence America was largely—mostly by choice—ignorant to, N.W.A.'s 'Straight Outta Compton' took America almost literally by storm in 1989. Selling over a million copies on word-of-mouth alone, the record was a product completely of its environment, but sought in the same time that it tried to represent the plagues facing its own hood to speak emblematically for those plaguing inner city communities across America. Silent until the dawn of the gangsta rap movement, irrefutably sparked on a national level by N.W.A., Dr. Dre took the lion share of the responsibility for creating the musical backdrop over which Ice Cube and M.C. Ren lyrically painted America's Nightmare for its largely suburban listeners.

Looking back over 15 years after the revolution of gangsta rap was first spawned by the group's seminal debut, Dr. Dre remarks humbly that "people today talk about how revolutionary N.W.A was and how we had all these big ideas about how to change rap…But we were just making it for the neighborhood…We were making stuff we knew our friends would like."

Elaborating on the latter, former group member and rap legend Ice Cube explained at the time of the album's release that "it's all about five brothers from the streets of Compton, tellin' it like it is. No shorts. We're just tellin' it exactly how it is, like a newspaper reporter. We don't water it down. It's like, if you saw somebody get shot, there's no one there to say this person got shot: 'Oh, you're not supposed to say that; that's a bad thing to do.' No...you just say what's goin' on. That's the same thing we do with our mouth, to the people. For the people who don't see or don't know, we become the vehicle to introduce it...Think about how you felt at that age...I was mad at everything. When I went to the schools in the Valley, going through those neighborhoods, seeing how different they were from mine, that angered me. The injustice of it, that's what always got me—the injustice."

While Dre wasn't counting on the national translation of his local ode to the neighborhood in the success of Straight Outta Compton, and the fact that Dr. Dre was called out in anthems like '8 Ball', where Eazy E raps that 'Dre makes the beat so God Damn funky', helped to cement the producer's own reputation overnight as one of the most cutting-edge in the game.

Even before 'Straight Outta Compton' was released, Dr. Dre was hard at work producing the group's debut underground LP, 1987's 'N.W.A. & the Posse' as well as group member Eazy E's debut LP, 'Eazy Does It', both of which heavily featured the D.O.C. from a writing standpoint. As Dre's best friend and future collaborator for the next six years, the history between Dr. Dre and D.O.C. is vitally important to any larger study of the producer's creative process as he and D.O.C. are inextricably linked from both a creative and commercial standpoint as it had to do with N.W.A.'s own evolution. This came mainly out of the fact that D.O.C. was responsible, along with Ice Cube, for penning many of the rhymes that other members of the group rapped on record. Moreover, it could be credibly argued that without D.O.C.'s assistance from a lyrical standpoint, the phenomenon that followed N.W.A.'s national rise to stardom might never have left Compton without the emcee.

Describing the roots of his and Dre's artistic kinship, D.O.C. observed that it was partly a matter of creative pragmatism on Dre's part to enlist D.O.C., such that "I think what Dre saw was my ability to help him make great records. Making a hit song for Eazy-E wasn't the easiest thing in the world. Eazy didn't have any rhythm, so it was hard to cross and besides I think Dre wanted to cross over his music so he could get it played on the radio. At that time they wasn't playin that gangsta shit on the radio. They wasn't trying to hear that, but if I could write songs for Eric that were gangsta, but not 'gangsta,' uh , I could have Eazy talkin' about all the gangsta shit in the world, but use words that don't scare white people. That's really all it was…Whenever you heard Eazy rappin', that was me, and then I stuck my own shit in like when Dre was doing the courtroom shit before 'Fuck the Police,' I was in there at the end. But to me it was more about making Eazy sound like he was the shit. That was my job, and I took that shit serious."

As D.O.C. recalls the evolution of N.W.A.'s sound and creative process leading up to the release of 'Straight Outta Compton', the emcee recalls an environment in which "(Dre and I first met through) a DJ from the West Coast who had just moved to Dallas. His name was Dr. Rock. He had a Saturday night mix show. Before he came to Dallas he was in a DJ group with Dr. Dre. That is how me and Dre met and ended up working together. Dre had came down here to be a guest DJ on this guy's show and Dre heard me rap and he pulled me to the side and told me in one of those classic Dr. Dre tones that I was the best muthafucka he had ever heard rapping. He said that I'd come back with him to California and that in a year we'd both be rich. And about six or seven months later, the shit ended up happening…NWA hadn't quite formed just yet. They were making records then, but it was real underground and it was real street so it wasn't concrete yet. As a matter of fact, right before I got there the original members of what was called NWA started breaking off and doing their own thing…The *Boys in tha Hood* record was just slowly starting to make noise underground, but the gel hadn't really come together yet…N.W.A. hadn't really got together yet. At least the group that the world knows as N.W.A. hadn't really all come together yet."

Continuing, D.O.C. explains that "when I got there everybody started finding their places. Everybody had their own individual skills, but Cube belonged to another group called C.I.A. at the time. Eazy was doing his own records at that time. Dre was just a producer, Ren was around and Dre worked with Yella. There was another dude around called Arabian Prince. All those guys was working with each other. Everybody was doing their own shit, but they all worked together. By the time I got there, guys really started taking that shit serious and they stopped fucking with Arabian Prince. Cube came from C.I.A. and left his other group alone. That's when we started doing work all together, but N.W.A. hadn't even really started working on its material. We all spent all our time trying to put Eazy's record together. I wrote about maybe 30 or 40 percent of that record. I wrote 'Still Talkin Shit,' I wrote 'We Want Eazy,' and more...Most of that early NWA shit I (helped) write. Songs like 'Boys in the Hood' and the four other songs that were done on the EP were done before I got there—'I Got My Radio' and a few others—but those were the only NWA songs that were done before I got there...I wrote all of Eazy's parts on the NWA records as well as being the extra set of ears for Dr. Dre because I was the only person that he really trusted. Back in those days Dre really trusted my ears...I was putting songs together in fuckin' 5 minutes back then. I can't remember one rap I wrote that Eazy didn't love, and muthafuckas in L.A. from Dre's relatives to Eazy's relatives to Cube's friends didn't love. Muthafuckas were like, 'D.O.C., you the shit!' Once they came in like that it was hard for me to come back to Texas because Texas never showed me that kind of love, but from the time I got off the plane in California, them muthafuckas was like, 'nigga you the shit.'...(After that), I was just a part of the team at that time. See, to me there was no difference between Eazy-E, N.W.A. or D.O.C. There was just titles that you put on a record. Like in my heart of hearts, you can't have an N.W.A. record without me, but anytime you see anything about N.W.A. in magazines they will never mention my name, but I was a pivotal part of that scene."

Prior to the string of hits that would follow between 1988 and 1991 prior to Dre leaving N.W.A. to go solo, in discussing the making of 'Straight Outta Compton', the producer recalls that he musically desired an organic sound that defied the popular trend of sampling that dominated rap at the time, such that, according to Dre, "most of my music has been played. Back when we started with the N.W.A. thing, it was a lot of drum loops, drum samples, and what have you. But if we were going to sample something, we would try to at least replay it, get musicians in and replay it. If it was something we couldn't replay, we would use the sample. I've tried to stay away from it as much as possible throughout my career from day one."

In describing the atmosphere during the making of the record, the L.A. Weekly reported that "Dre and Yella shared the producer's credit. They were almost always the first ones in the Torrance studio and the last to leave. Others came and went as needed or whim dictated. It was clear (Dre) was in charge."

In spite of their later extremely public feud upon Dre's exit from N.W.A., Dre's former bandmate Eazy E recalls that he knew at the time he formed N.W.A. with Dre that the group's sound never would have morphed without Dre, such that "Dre came from the Wrecking Crew, but I got him to do this other type of music I wanted to do, the gangsta shit, and I got Dre away from what he was doing…Here's what Dre did…Dre was good at putting it together. So we might have an idea for a song…(then) Dre would put it together…You could tell if you knew Dre (and) his style."

DJ and producing partner Yella explained Dre's side of their production process and team as one in which "me and Dre did all the recording. Dre did most of the beats but you know it was like a group thing." Clique member and longtime Dre collaborator the D.O.C. recalls that "Yella was sorta the technical kind of dude. He understood the machines that these guys worked on. He knew them backwards and forwards. He was great with the tape machines, drum machines, and boards. I'll put it to you like this. I considered myself to be another pair of ears in the studio when Dre was working. Well, if I was another pair of ears, then Yella was another pair of hands. It's hard to make a great record by yourself man. There will always be at least 5 great musicians together to make a classic record. That's what we had with NWA's records."

Elaborating on the genesis of the group's sound, Yella recalled that "on the first maxi-single, before the Straight Outta Compton album, Cube was in school in Arizona for a year. So me, Ren, Dre, and Eazy worked the whole single promotion-wise for a whole year. Cube had a scholarship or something so he was gone. The four of us put in a lot of free hours before we made the actual album. Cube was writing a lot of Eazy's stuff that Eazy didn't like because it wasn't him, he wasn't a rapper! We liked Eazy because originally, he had the money, but also because the sound of his voice sold. He sounded and looked like a little kid. That's why we pushed him out front; he was the image. When you thought of NWA, you thought of Eazy-E first. It was just a look. (Dre and) I was always in the background through all the production and everything...Ice-T was rapping but some people didn't know where he was from. Some people thought he was from New York. He had a different style from us. We were almost the first ones to cuss on a rap record, because that's how we talk so I think we started 'street music' first. We were just different from him. NWA started a legend and that legend has now opened the doors for all these gangsta rappers or whatever you want to call them. We didn't think of it as gangsta rap. To us, it was just street music. We rapped about what we knew…NWA was really about street music. I don't think NWA started West Coast, but I think we made the name for it. We was rapping about what we lived around, saw and what could happen. We was talking about real stuff in the ghetto, and that ghetto can be any ghetto, not just Compton…Nothing phony; we just rapping about real living. We never changed in that respect, even when we began to cross over."

Once Ice Cube rejoined the fold, the production of Straight Outta Compton was still underway and far from done. Explaining how the group's creative process evolved in constructing any of the many classics that would define the album upon completion, Cube explained that "here's how we break down a song: Dre and Yella do a beat…Alright, then, and I say 'Yo, man, I got a verse for that.' Then up comes Eazy and he has a verse. Then we do our little tricks on the break. So we put all these things together and we got a record. Like on 'Fuck The Police,' everybody did their own little flavor. Eazy-E wrote his part, Ren wrote his, we all used our own perspective on the subject of fuck the police…Instead of sitting down together and working things out and having somebody say, 'Naw, man, I don't think you should write that,' you know what I'm saying? What I'm saying is this man, think. Let him write what he thinks. Let me write what I think. So we never really criticize each other's record."

Co-producer MC Yella explained that "me and Dre did all the recording. Dre did most of the beats but you know it was like a group thing. It wasn't like this person did everything. You know Dre is Dre…I've been knowing him forever. He's the best producer out there now in the rap industry."

Fellow group member and co-lead emcee MC Ren meanwhile recalled that "Dre was like the main ear…He'd tell you,

'Try to make it like this.' You'd do it. He'd be like, 'Cool.' Or, 'That's terrible.' Dre'd look at you like, you dumb mother fucker."

Dre would summarize his work during the N.W.A. period as one in which he hallmarked a signature style, which the producer likened analogously to "your Richard Pryors in the world and your Bill Cosbys. My mother let me listen to Richard Pryor when I was a kid. You know what I'm saying? And it was funny to me, the shock value and all. It's just like 'Pulp Fiction.' I don't understand how people can love that movie and then say my records are bad. My records are straight-up dark comedy…I love hard-core hip-hop…That's what I'm good at."

Dre's production instincts would pay off for the group, as 'Straight Outta Compton' was both a critical and commercial success, with *Rolling Stone Magazine* for one example remarking in their 5-Star 1989 review that the album was instantly "one of hip-hop's crucial albums", making specific note of "Dr. Dre's busy funk production (which lends) the proceedings a carefree, unhinged air."

The Source, meanwhile, would later proclaim that "Dr. Dre's production genius was undeniable." Ironically, despite the fact that the album launched his career, Dre claims that "to this day I can't stand that album, I threw that thing together in six weeks so we could have something to sell out of the trunk."

In a summary review of the album's overall place in Dre's broader catalog in context of the point in the history of his career to come, the *L.A. Weekly* commented that "the fast-beat Wreckin' Cru techno is absent, replaced by slower, deeper, funkier rhythm tracks set in a scrap heap soundscape of sirens, gunshots, shouts, curses and cars. The overall effect can be ominous…The results do not match Dre's later musical sophistication; few things do."

"The D.O.C. is a large, graceful man who was once among the world's best rappers—he played the English language the way Itzhak Perlman plays a Strad—until his career was cut short by a freak automobile accident that crushed his throat and left him unable to rap."

—*Rolling Stone Magazine*

Chapter 4
No One Can Do It Better— Dr. Dre & D.O.C.

Arguably the greatest shooting star of the 1980s rap scene, the D.O.C.'s rise and fall is among the most tragic of hip hop's up to the point of the murder of Tupac Shakur. It wasn't a change in trends that robbed him of his chance at super stardom, which he'd surely have achieved based on the success of his debut. Rather, the details of the car accident that crushed his larynx are widely known in the annals of hip hop folklore, but what he is truly remembered and acknowledged for is the seminal solo album he released in 1989 on Ruthless Records, the aptly titled 'No One Can Do It Better.'

This album was equally as important for Dr. Dre as he stepped out of the shadows of his N.W.A. bandmates as the record's sole producer. The futuristic sonics of the album alone made it landmark, but it also showcased Dre for the first time in a light where people could appreciate his singular abilities as the most cutting-edge producer of the late 1980s.

In *Rolling Stone Magazine's* review of the album, they remarked that D.O.C. & Dre had "produced an incredible '89 debut which was appropriately titled *No One Can Do It Better*. Armed with a vicious vocabulary and seriously hot Dre beats, the D.O.C. came with a slew of classic tracks including 'The Formula', 'Let The Bass Go' and 'The Grand Finale', a sizzling posse cut with N.W.A."

According to D.O.C., his artistic rendezvous with Dre seemed destined even before the two first met, explaining that "it was so funny and so spiritual how it all came together. When Dre was in a group called the World Class Wreckin' Crew—this was before I met Dre, I met Dre later on—Dre had a song on one of the Wreckin' Crew albums called 'Surgery.' My given name is Tracy and my friends call me Tray. When that song came out whenever we were playing around that's what people would say, Dr. Dre. When I started rapping, I used to call myself Dr. T. Then T went to Doc T. When I finally got with NWA I figured we're all in this bitch together if y'all got periods then I got periods. Y'all N.W.A., now I'm D.O.C."

In the beginning of D.O.C.'s career and affiliation with Dre, it was a common misconception that the emcee was a member of the group, which N.W.A. co-producer Yella corrected at the time by explaining that "D.O.C. wasn't no member he was just a writer, he was part of the clique but he wasn't an actual NWA member."

The point of D.O.C.'s affiliation with N.W.A. centered in his creative partnership and kindred artistic spirit with Dr. Dre, such that out of the writing D.O.C. did for N.W.A., he and Dre were inspired to branch out on their own to create the rapper's seminal debut, 'No One Can Do It Better.' The transition was natural, as D.O.C. remembers it, "after we put out the Eazy E record and the *NWA Straight Outta Compton* we started working on my record. It was the natural progression. I was the best thing that we had in that camp, so that's what we were going to put out…I am a solo act. I'm not a member of that group…although I am, I'm not. I was meant to be a solo artist in this bitch. My time was coming and when it came I was going to go home and start my own situation like NWA. That was my plan."

The D.O.C.'s artistic confidence was reinforced—both lyrically and musically—through his partnership with creative muse Dr. Dre, explaining that "me and Dr. Dre, were an anomaly. Like Dre could have made a whole beat record with no guitars, no bass, and I could have made raps for all those beats and still would have made a great record. What Dre does is make shit that you could see in your head when it's playing. He knows how to bring drama. He knows how to take it away and leave it all up to the artist. He knows how to sometimes just make it quiet. I mean that dude's pretty god damn good."

Dr. Dre in the Studio

Where the two had spent years writing and producing hits for others, it was finally time to break out on their own, with D.O.C. recalling that the collaboration was a matter of mutual respect and reciprocal ambition, such that "I remember Mel-Man telling me one time that he asked Dre who was the best to rap on top of his beats and Mel-Man told me that Dre said it was me, and I can pretty much believe that because I am one of the few muthafuckas that loved, and I don't mean I like it as in when I hear it I wanna dance, but I *loved* Dr. Dre's production. So that means when it stinks we need to fix it, because I love it. Not in the terms where it's something that I like, but it's something that I want to be great and I wanted him to be great. I always wanted Dre to be Quincy Jones. At least in this hip-hop thing, I wanted him to be Russell Simmons. I didn't want him to just be satisfied with being Dr. Dre, hit-maker or beat-maker. The guy has the potential to be huge in this world. I mean he's a smart guy with a good heart, and I think he's got the best ears in the business today."

The fact the duo had each other's backs to the degree they did allowed for a creative trust to exist that was based on a relationship that D.O.C. described as "the closest thing that you could have to a brother because we fought and argued like family. That's the kind of person I am. I'm a real southern kind of person, so if I have love for you and if something's in my heart, then I'm gonna express myself. There ain't no gangsta shit. I don't wanna beat yo ass, I don't wanna shoot you in your ass, or none of that shit. I just want you to think about what I'm sayin' and try to do right. At the same time, show business was around us and everybody was just blowin' up in their own way, and you know how show business can really get muthafuckas' heads fucked up…(We just had) fun man. That's the only word I got for that. The shit was so much fun because at that time when I moved to California, I

Chapter 4. No One Can Do It Better— Dr. Dre & D.O.C.

moved at Dr. Dre's urging. Once I got there I had to stay with this dude's brother by Centennial High School for like a month or 2, and then Dre got his own apartment. Him and Yella got an apartment, so I spent all day everyday with Dre for those first 3 or 4 years, I was with this guy all day everyday. We slept in the same house, we ate at the same time. We drove to work together in the same beat up little Toyota Corolla…Me and Dre were really in sync. Like I go good with his ear. Not just his beats, I can hear the kind of shit that he hears, but still I'm able to hear my own shit in it."

Delving into the process of creating 'No One Can Do It Better' in the studio, D.O.C. explains that conceptually, "every song (on) the 'No One Can Do It Better' album was just me being me, and Dre being Dre. We had no plans. We just had fun and did the shit, and when we felt like we had enough, we quit. 'How many is that?' '17?' 'Yeah, that's enough, fuck it, let's move on.' Ironically relaxed in its creation considering how seriously the industry took the album upon its release, D.O.C. explains that there was no joking around with the artistic merits of the music they created, such that "when you mess around with a DOC song then what you're basically getting is a book that lasts about four minutes. It's a story. It has to have a beginning, a middle and an end. It has to all tie together. It's just like a movie whether it be a drama, a comedy or a comeback story like *Rocky*. Everybody wants Rocky to win. Go Rocky. He was beating the shit outta Mr. T and we didn't give a fuck about Mr. T. And we Black! We was suppose to been saying kick his ass, but we want Rocky to win, because that's a part of the story…I was one of the muthafuckas that set the blueprint."

One of the most impressive elements of the album's production was the infusion of various music styles that crossed naturally over one another without boundary, evident for instance with the rock-driven track 'Beautiful but Deadly', which D.O.C. described as "Dr. Dre's idea. Traditionally I'm a East Coast rapper, so he felt what Run and them was doing back then, uh, well we felt that I could do that kind of thing. Crossover into a Rock n' Roll kind of theme and not really skip a beat or lose any of my hardcore audience doing it. Because of the type of rapper that I was. But it really wasn't straight Rock n' Roll because that's a old Parliament song, and Dre is a Parliament freak."

Elaborating on the former, one of the most impressive elements of 'No One Can Do It Better' was the variety of song styles reflected in each individual track, but originally spun in Dre and D.O.C.'s own magical interpretation, such that, for instance, with 'Its Funky Enough', the album's reggae-driven first single, D.O.C. describes a process of creation in which he was "sittin' at the turntable listening to a song called 'Misdemeanor' by The Silvers, and I loved it. It was a funky little thing. It was the shit, but Dr. Dre said there is nothing I can sample. I'm not fucking with it. A couple of days later I'm back in the studio and I pull that muthafucka back out and I'm listening to it, and I ask him again. He said, there is not enough space or some shit, and that he can't sample the record so he can't use it. I let it go again. Well we came back in there, and I think it was like a week later, and I got the record and I was playing with it, and I had to beg this guy to make the fuckin' beat. He says 'Okay fuck it, I'll make it.' He put the shit down and I was gonna write another rap to it, but the way he was clowning me behind it I said, 'Fuck it, Ill just put this rap that I got on it, then we can work it out if it ain't right.' I had been drinkin' some beer, and smokin' some weed with Laylaw on the other side of the studio. So that when I got back inside the studio I was feelin' kind of good and the beat sounded like some Jamaican shit to me after Dre finished fucking with it. That was the reason why I rapped it the way

Chapter 4. No One Can Do It Better— Dr. Dre & D.O.C.

that I rapped it, because it wasn't designed to be like that…I had been in there drinking all day, so when I got under the headphones the shit sounded Jamaican. Dre went like, 'Since you're in the booth why don't you go on and give us a level on it?' I said to myself, since the shit sound Jamaican, I'm gonna give it a Jamaican feel because it sounds Jamaican to me. I did the whole song in one take and we never changed it…I did that muthafuckin' song one time through, thinkin' that we were gonna go back and do it over again, and Dre was like 'Fuck that, that was a one take willy…I always thought that the song had a Jamaican feel to it."

Perhaps the track most ahead of its time on 'No One Can Do It Better' was the straight sonic-science of 'The Formula', which became a hit single and video, and sounded like the soundtrack to a dream upon first listen. Ironically, the song came to BOTH Dre and the D.O.C. out of a dream, such that "Dr. Dre and Michel'Le went somewhere and they didn't make it back home till about 1:30 or maybe 2 o'clock in the morning. Now me I'm straight outta Texas. I ain't got a pot to piss in, or a window to throw it out of, so when they go out I'm just at the house on the floor. Well I was sleepin' when he came back in, and he said, 'Nigga, I was on my way home and I got caught up in a day dream, it was me and you was bustin' a song called 'Tha Formula' to a Marvin Gaye beat!' He went in there and he got a tape and he played me the Marvin Gaye song and he went in there and went to sleep. Well me, I stayed up from about 2 o'clock till about 5:30 maybe finishing that song and we did that song the next day."

Sadly, for all its brilliance, 'The Formula' would inadvertently contribute to the tragically premature end of the D.O.C.'s rise to national prominence via a violent car accident that crushed his larynx. As the rapper explains, "we were doing two videos, 'The Formula' video and the 'Beautiful but

Deadly' video one weekend. It was like eighteen hour days for both videos. It was like being at a party for two days straight and then trying to drive home drunk—that's really what happened—and I didn't make it. What's really funny about that particular video, 'The Formula,' was me being put together from pieces in some hospital and the next day…That's some crazy shit for real."

The *Source Magazine* would later acknowledge Dre through its review of the album as "being the principle architect of N.W.A's menacing, groundbreaking West Coast sound through much of the late '80's and early 90's…Dr. Dre was also an influential talent broker, whose 1989 introduction of Texas-born lyricist the D.O.C.… the platinum album's barrage of groove-heavy live guitar, drums and keyboard synthesizers allowed space for his authoritative vocal presence to shine. ('It's Funky Enough')… (Along) with the extensive writing credits on The Chronic, 'No One Can Do It Better' remains an influential work revered by hardcore rap aficionados."

Ultimately, whether they knew it or not at the time, 'No One Can Do It Better' was an artistic overture on Dre's part to what would become the Chronic, in terms of giving listeners

Chapter 4. No One Can Do It Better—Dr. Dre & D.O.C.

a glimpse of the future he envisioned aurally for hip hop. Thankfully for D.O.C., his bond with Dre was strong enough that when both left Ruthless Records a year later, they left together. Moreover, it was actually D.O.C.'s relationship with Suge Knight prior to Dre ever knowing him that would serve as the catalyst for creating the greatest independent hip hop powerhouse of the 1990s.

As D.O.C. explained the genesis of Death Row, while he had lost his chance at sustained rap superstardom, he still had people whispering in his ear for him to continue, which D.O.C. felt was unrealistic given his predicament. What he did see in the way of a future for himself in the business was a continued creative collaboration with Dre in which D.O.C. would serve primarily as a writer for other artists, as he had in the early Ruthless days.

According to the rapper, "Sylvia Rhone, she's the big wig at Elektra, who I was signed to through Ruthless, was encouraging me, as well as Jerry Heller and Eazy E, to keep going. You gotta make another record. I felt that my confidence in myself had been diminished because of the golden throat—I was the kid with golden voice, I said it in my records. That was the crowning thing, my vocal tone. I could do things with my voice that you can't even imagine. And I hadn't begun to show you anything yet. Man, I had more confidence than I had brains. But after the accident Dre said to me one day that if it were up to him, he wouldn't do it. He said, 'DOC, them muthafuckas call you the greatest ever and I'd go out like that." Hearing those words from Dre, who is the person I most respected in the music business period, when he said that it made sense to me. I know when he said that shit, he's not speaking from jealousy or envy. He's not speaking from a plastic place, he really cares about me. He's giving me the real shit, the shit that I really don't want to hear. I heard him and I understood. He said, 'You got a really good thing going up here. You're writing all these songs that are worth a lotta money. Keep your ass up in here and keep working until you figure out what the fuck you want to do.' So that's what I did...Well I asked Dre what he thought, and he said that if it was him, he wouldn't make another record. He said they think your the king right now and that's how I would go out. I had so much faith in Dre, that when Dre said that then that was it. There was no more rappin' for me. Now I'm gonna use my writing ability to help us be the shit because that's really what I always wanted. It wasn't about no money to me. I just wanted to be the greatest. I wasn't trying to get rich out there with these guys, even though I did. I mean I wanted the fame and the fortune and all that, but I wanted when muthafuckas said my name, I wanted it to be unequivocal that this guy D.O.C. is the greatest."

Beginning to envision his own artistic future post-accident, D.O.C. had the benefit of Suge's business savvy to help guide his direction, and inadvertently, Dre's as well. The end result

Chapter 4. No One Can Do It Better— Dr. Dre & D.O.C.

would be the healthiest possible creative working environment for Dre to further blossom as a producer, and a much more financially secure one in the same time where the fruits of his labor were concerned. Explaining the genesis of the eventual partnership between Dre and Suge Knight—and in essence that of Dre's evolution to the next level of his career—D.O.C. explained that "me and Suge had been working together for a while…He was more like a friend of mine. They say he was a bodyguard, but I never paid the muthafucka no money for body guarding me. He was just a friend really, a guy who hung around. We went places, we kicked it. We had started trying to do business together right before the wreck…You know Suge didn't have to come to my hospital bed everyday. I wasn't paying him. He didn't know at that time we were gonna go make Death Row…I talked Suge into getting him up there and we were going to start our own thing…I was trying to start a label with Suge Knight. I had an office in Beverly Hills, but I was going through issues after that car wreck. I was trying to find myself and we felt like we needed Dre in order to make that shit work…We had already went through my little contract, Suge and I and other lawyers and found out that I was not fairly being compensated. With that information, I went to Dre and I started having conversations with him about he and I doing our own thing. If Eazy's fucking me, then he's probably doing it to you too. He's fucking Cube and dada dada da. I just got those kinds of dialogue started."

Convincing Dre to leave was another story entirely. Through his affiliation with Suge, Dre and D.O.C. went through much the same experience Ice Cube did of having the wool pulled back from their eyes regarding Ruthless' shady business dealings. As the rapper recalls, "when we looked into Dre's shit, sure enough, his shit was kinda flimsy too. Now what Eazy should have did at that point, he should've said,

Dr. Dre in the Studio

'OK Dre, fuck this shit. What we need to do is get in this muthafucka and start it over and make it up so we're all happy and we all breaking bread.' But no, what Eazy did was the classic nigga thing. He said hey, this is my shit and I don't give a fuck. It's gone go like it's gone go. But what that did was separate Eazy E and Dre. Now that's really all that Suge and me needed to get Dre to come on in where we at because Dre knew that a lot of that creative shit came outta me. He knew that he's not gonna be able to sit in the studio with Eric and come up with this shit. So he comes over here and we get the idea that we gonna start our own label. We're gone split the shit 50/50. And Suge is gonna help us administrate and do business. That's where all of that shit started from…We started having meetings with this guy Dick Griffy, who was like an older Suge. I've heard stories about Dick Griffy being the big bad wolf during his day. So him and Suge were just like old generation/new generation of the same nigga, but shark niggas. Not just big bad, beat-up-everybody niggas like folks in the magazines would have you to believe, but the muthafuckas are sharks. They on their Ps and Qs. They got good business sense. They know how to deal with the powers that be, because the music business is a big, big, big game. And trust me, they'll never tell you the ins and outs, but there are a few niggas who know. Well, Dick Griffy was one of them kinda niggas who knew and Suge was an up-and-comin nigga like that…Dre didn't leave Ruthless because Suge went and found him and showed him some funny shit in his contract, he left Ruthless because I asked him to. He left Ruthless because I wanted us to go and make our own label. Mine and his because we were the ones putting in all the work."

Needless to say, Dre's departure from Ruthless Records all but crippled the label, to the point where, according to MC Ren, "when Dre left it was like all that shit fell apart. Eric wanted to do another album (NWA) without Dre…first u got to

Chapter 4. No One Can Do It Better— Dr. Dre & D.O.C.

look at it like we had already done another album without Cube and it was successful it was like when Cube left the public was like 'Can they do it without Cube?' so we did a 100 miles and runnin and Niggaz 4life and that proved it. Classic…you know what I mean. but after Dre if Dre wasn't doin the beats I didn't see that it could go down, so I was like I don't wanna do it. Eric wanted to do it and bring new producers and shit. So we had a fallout for like a couple of years over that…we didn't even talk."

Yella, Dre's production partner from the past 6 years, agreed that the departure put the company into a state of disarray, including testing Yella's own sense of loyalty, and pitting the latter he held for Ruthless against that of his loyalty to Dre, such that "Dre and I was like brothers. We was tight, real tight," Yella said. "Them first few years we was all like family. Even when Cube left, the rest of us was like family…I remember when Dre told me he was leaving NWA and invited me to leave with him."

At the time of his exit from Ruthless to head out on his own, Dre had a major impact on sculpting what had become the West Coast hip hop thus far. He pretty much single-handedly steered Ruthless from the first gangsta single, Eazy-E's 'Boyz-n-the-Hood,' J.J. Fad's simple-minded novelty hit 'Supersonic' and N.W.A's 'Fuck the Police' to a hip-hop diva album for a girlfriend, Michel'le, and the ghetto Gotterdammerung of N.W.A's *Niggaz4life*, which shocked America when it topped the pop charts. Dre caught the moment pretty well.

Dre didn't get the credit he did at the time because there was no one else there to give it out to, rather there was no one else on his level to acknowledge because he had no competition.

35

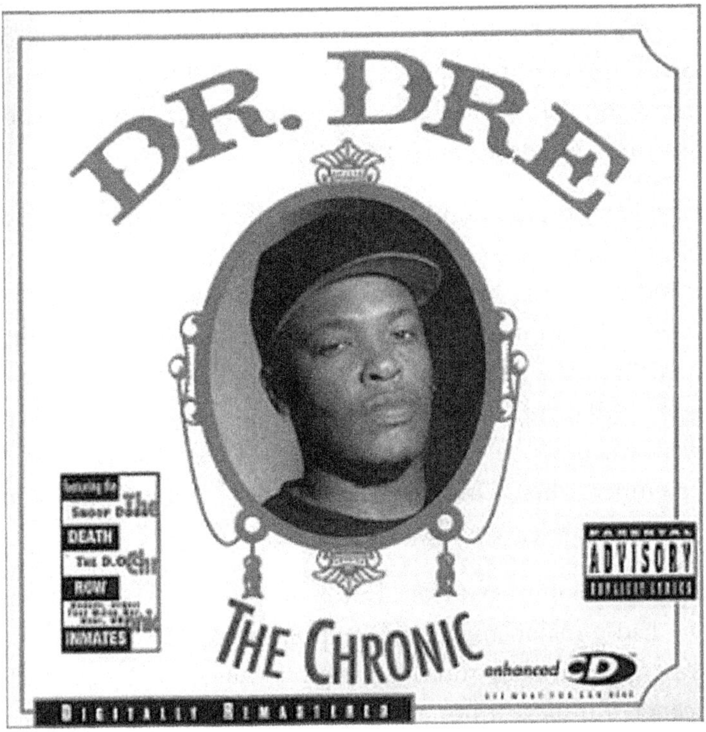
DR. DRE
THE CHRONIC
DEATH
ROW
INMATES
PARENTAL ADVISORY
enhanced CD
DIGITALLY REMASTERED

"The Chronic (was) an untouchable masterpiece of California Gangsta Rap. Chock full of Parliament/Funkadelic bass lines, high-pitched synths, and lolo-rockin' beats, track after track of G-Funk gems propelled the album to the top of the charts, made Snoop Dogg a household name, and changed the sound of hip-hop forever."

—*Rolling Stone Magazine*

Chapter 5
The Chronic

Much in the way the club crowds were moving hypnotically along to Dre's beats as the 1990s unfolded, it seemed too that the commercial tides of the times were helpless but to turn with the changes Dre had in mind for hip hop's mainstream as he began conceptualizing what became 'The Chronic.' Within Dre's own inner circle, a small mass of people seemed eager to follow him from Ruthless onto Death Row, or anywhere else he wanted to be, in an atmosphere that D.O.C. described as "people close to the circle because of Dre. Most of the people who came to that circle came because they wanted to be around Dre for what he could do."

Dre's partner in what became Death Row Records, Suge Knight, perhaps in seeking to weed out some of the aforementioned hangers-on, had a business blueprint to match Dre's sonic, one that dictated that anyone involved on the creative side with Death Row be there only because they had something to offer. Dre was hungry—both for commercial and financial success—as was Suge for the latter, and the Chronic would lay the foundation for a powerhouse.

Neither Dre nor Knight viewed success as a competition that had room for a second place price, and in seizing their prize, they enlisted a team of players who were equally as hungry, and willing to do whatever was necessary to make Death Row what it became soon thereafter. As Suge recalled at the time, "to have a vision, and believe in something, you gonna work hard at it. When I had my vision with the music business, my whole motive was to work hard and be the best at it. So I treated it like we was a football team. My background is athletics, far as being athletic, and being on a football team. So I looked at it like, well, (Death Row's) gonna be like a training camp. Having the artists, having the producers, having the writers, having everybody together. Where they eat together, and damn near sleep together, and they work together. And the chemistry's gonna sound better because the album's gonna be much fuller. Instead of an artist talking about me, me, me, me, its gonna be about a variety of different things going on."

The result of Knight's blueprint was Dr. Dre's landmark The Chronic, completed in the latter half of 1991, and released in November of that year. Its impact would change the face of hip hop permanently, and chart much of the operating course for independent hip hop labels in the latter 1990s. The Chronic, in its commercial definition, referred to a grade of marijuana leaf that was considered an instant classic among those who smoked it, requiring only a single hit to reach a buzz. A similar metaphor applied to the success of the album, in that it only took one listen before rap fans nationwide were hooked, thus making Death Row's first release an instant classic, in line, metaphorically, with the effect of its title.

Chapter 5. The Chronic

In describing his creative inspiration for hip hop's first official concept album—perhaps apart from 'Straight Outta Compton', Dre explained that "back in the 70s that's all people were doing: getting high, wearing Afros, bell-bottoms and listening to Parliament-Funkadelic. That's why I called my album The Chronic and based my music and the concepts like I did: because his shit was a big influence on my music. Very big." With the making of the Chronic, which Suge bankrolled to the reported tune of $750,000, Dre was given for the first time the opportunity to make the album that he felt 'Straight Outta Compton' could have been, but couldn't become due to its budgetary and technological constraints.

As D.O.C. explained it, Dre's rationale, "(the Chronic was) the dopest hip-hop record of all time. 'Straight Outta Compton' could have been the greatest, but it was so raw and hard that it didn't give you no time to fuckin' party and shit. With 'The Chronic' that's all you did and you never knew what was coming next. With all the NWA records, after a while you kind of got an idea of what was gonna happen next." As more or less Dre's defensive guard in the studio, D.O.C. contributed heavily to the writing of the Chronic, and also played a mentoring role of sorts for the younger artists newly signed to Death Row's stable, like Snoop Dogg and Daz and Kurupt among others, coaching them on how to write hits, and holding the young artists to a standard in which "I (didn't) allow them to write bullshit. I listen with a loving ear, that means I want you to be the shit and everything less just ain't civilized."

Describing for his own part, the atmosphere that surrounded the making of the Chronic, Dre explained at the time that "everybody who walks has something he or she can do in the studio…Every person walking has some kind of talent that they can get on tape. I can take anybody who reads this

39

magazine and make a hit record on him. You don't have to rap. You can do anything. You can go into the studio and talk. I can take a fuckin' 3-year-old and make a hit record on him. God has blessed me with this gift…Sometimes it feels good for me to be able to mold an artist and get him a hit record and to show him something that was inside of him that he didn't know about. It feels good to me. Everybody in the business has called me to try and do some tracks, but I can't see myself doing anything for somebody who already has money, you know. I get more joy out of getting somebody like Snoop. And it excites the shit out of me to see the reaction on a new artist's face when he gets asked for his first autograph. I tell Snoop all the time: He is going to be the biggest shit, Snoop is going to be the biggest thing to black people since the straightening comb."

Recalling his own reaction and excitement to Snoop's presence during the recording of the Chronic, D.O.C. explained that "When Snoop came in, he was great. He had all the tools in him to be what he is right now, but he didn't have the desire and nobody was there to push him. That was my job. You have to be able to communicate with everybody, not just muthafuckas in Long Beach, and not just muthafuckas in L.A. So that means your subject matter may have to switch, your wordplay may have to change a little bit. You know just give us all something that we can love on."

Elaborating on Dre's production process during the early Death Row days, the D.O.C. described an environment in which "the formula (was): took 2 of the major components from the Chronic days with me and Colin Wolfe, and moved them over (to Death Row) and that's really what it was. Colin was a musician so Dre would say 'Play,' and Colin would play. Sooner or later he would come up on a couple of chords that we all liked so, uh, I'll give you a perfect example. 'Deep

Chapter 5. The Chronic

Cover,' the guy was just playin' the 4 notes and Dre said 'Wait a minute keep playin' that.' That baseline was Colin Wolfe's shit. Dre added the drum the piano hit and that was it, that was the song."

Speaking specifically on the Chronic recording sessions, D.O.C. recalls that "(that) was the most fun that I have ever had on a record. Snoop brought a vibe to the music that wasn't there before. If there was levels to the game, let's say NWA stayed intact and I never had the accident. The next level would be Snoop. That was the only way you could come and totally fuck everybody up because when you the youngest you always gonna fuck it up, and he was the young one at the time. Now let me get this point straight first. I would have forever been Marvin Gaye, god dammit. When I opened up my mouth, it would have been nothing but jewelry, but when Snoop came, me being the type of person that I am I would have had so much love for him and put so much energy into his shit the same way I did that he would have had no choice but to be the shit…We were there everyday and there is no better place to be than the studio. That's where all the weed at. That's where the drinks is at, and niggaz is doing they thang. Besides, I took it very personal that these guys wouldn't make bullshit around me. I remember when Dre first started making the beat to 'Dre Day.' He had a lot of shit missing and it was certain things that he was doing and I was like, 'That sounds like a load of shit.' He says 'OK we'll wait till' tomorrow.' By the time I got to the studio the next day that muthafucka was bangin.'…When you're in the studio with Dre, that shit that's on tape is what's in his mind…When you make a classic record the majority of the time it's just fun. That's all it is. Like the *Straight Outta Compton* record, the Eazy record, the *Chronic* record, the 2001 record and now this record I'm doing right now, it all follows the same formula—just having fun and don't settle

41

Dr. Dre in the Studio

for shit that ain't the shit. I don't give a fuck if you're my greatest friend, while we in the studio all I wanna hear is dope shit. If you ain't bringing dope shit to the table then goddamn it you need to move over and let somebody else bring it. We're trying to make hits around this muthafucka. That was our saying back in the beginning, all hits and no bullshit. That's what we want."

Dr. Dre's inherent style of producing—was very much like a TEXAS football training camp in which the producer explains that "I'm a very good motivator…I direct well. I'm a person that will spend three or four hours working on one line of a song to get it correct. I have to be able to work with artists who are ready to go through that torture."

Dogg Pound member and Death Row artist Kurupt recalled that Dre's strict production etiquette was one in which "if he didn't like something you did, then that was it: You were out. If he did like, you're in." Still, as tough a coach as he may have been, Dre made no effort to hide his own excitement over the phenomenon his sound was having on the industry, enthusing at the time to a journalist that "the music is just in me now, you know. That's the only thing I can say. People ask me how I come up with these hits, and I can only say that I know what I like, and I'm quick to tell a motherfucker what I don't like and know what people like to play in their cars...Snoop is going to be the shit, watch."

It was as obvious to everyone in the Death Row camp as it was to the rest of the world that Snoop would take Dre as a producer and Death Row as a label to entirely new heights, such that as label mate D.O.C. observed, "well by that time Snoop was coastin. Snoop was on cruise control, all cylinders were clicking and you knew what it was gonna be. If I remember right, they were playing this guy's album on the radio way before it came out. That's how bad muthafuckas wanted it. Playing it will all the curses and finding ways to bleep that shit out. I remember the night that that niggaz shit came on sale. There was lines around the block in Century City. It was a great follow up to 'The Chronic.' It was a classic follow up to a classic record."

For Dr. Dre, the Chronic established a new revolution in the record industry, putting gangsta rap on the map as a corporate force, and put him in the pilot seat steering its sound into the 1990s. It was easy, and even exciting, for critics to acknowledge and celebrate Dre's influence over the genre as it had come full circle throughout the latter 1980s. The Dre sound was clean but edgy, deeply funky, featuring slow, big-bottomed, slightly dirty beats and powered by guitar and bass work that was not sampled but recreated in the studio. Unlike East Coast rap productions, the fidelity of the final product was not inflected by the fidelity of scratchy R&B records that had been played too many times. It was Dre's production work—on Eazy-E, on N.W.A, on rap legend D.O.C., on Pomona group Above the Law, on Snoop Doggy Dogg, on himself—that made gangsta rap among the most vital pop genres to come along in the last few years.

It had become common knowledge that "Dre's lovely, funk-laden, Cali-scorched beats on 'The Chronic' set a standard for production that had never been exceeded…This ode to California living had become one of the greatest hip-hop albums ever created. Still, heading into 1993, Dre was hungrier than ever to continue the evolution of his G-Funk revolution, remarking at the time that 'I did record The Chronic in 1992…The year was not a total loss.'"

"Virtually every song on Snoop's debut is a classic... Unfortunately, nobody makes music like this anymore."

—*The Source*

Chapter 6
Doggystyle

On the outset of the release of *Doggy Style*, it was clear that 'The Chronic' had already changed the face of hip hop permanently, and that 'Doggystyle' was set to do what no 'gangsta' rap album had ever done before—both in commercial sales numbers and in terms of crossover. Dr. Dre publicly stated his desire to outdo the success of his own debut album, which had served to introduce Snoop Dogg to the hip hop world, with the release of Snoop's solo LP. At the time, Snoop for his part remarked that "when some writer asked him why it was taking so long to get my album out, Dre was quoted as saying that the tracks he was doing for me were 'the future of funk.'"

Picking up where Snoop left off, as they often did in rhymes, Dre qualified the latter by explaining that "I've never heard the perfect hip-hop album, but I'd like to make one. *The Chronic* is about the closest. Public Enemy's *Nation of Millions* was dope as hell. Eric B and Rakim, their first album, I really liked a lot, and Boogie Down Productions, *Criminal Minded* was def...Did you see all those reels that are in the studio?...There's 35 or 36 reels of Snoop in there...Each reel holds three songs. So far, I have five that I like. That's just a small example of...how deep I'm going into this album. I feel that the tracks that I'm doing for him right now are the future of the funk."

Rolling Stone Magazine, in one of its many profiles of Dr. Dre, Snoop Dogg and Death Row throughout the early 1990s—reflecting their massive influence and phenomenon over the industry—gave a fascinating insight into Dre's production style as it had evolved by 1993 in one article, describing a process in which "listening to a Dre beat take shape in the studio is like watching a snowball roll downhill in a Bugs Bunny cartoon, taking on mass as it goes. Dre may find something he likes from an old drum break, loop it and gradually replace each part with a better tom-tom sound, a kick-drum sound he adores, until the beat bears the same relationship to the original that the Incredible Hulk does to Bill Bixby…Dre scratches in a sort of surfadelic munching noise, and then from his well-stocked Akai MPC60 sample comes a shriek, a spare piano chord, an ejaculation from the first Beastie's record—'Let me clear my throat'—and the many-layered groove is happening, bumping, breathing, almost loud enough to see…Dre…twists a few knobs on the Moog and comes up with the synthesizer sound so familiar from *The Chronic*, almost on pitch but not quite, sliding a bit between notes. The people in the crowded control room bob their heads to the beat in unison."

The whole world was watching Dre, not just in admiration of the sound he was creating, but as well for cues as to where he would next direct the genre he had almost single-handedly founded. It was in this time that Dre's ear for discovering new talent also began to gain acknowledgement. Through his mentoring, Ice Cube and the D.O.C., considered by many alongside Rakim to be two of the most gifted and profound lyricists of the 1980s, had emerged. As the architect of N.W.A.'s sound, Dre had also been credited to some degree with introducing them to the world.

Now, with Snoop Doggy Dogg on the verge of international stardom, Dre was laying the groundwork for longevity that went well beyond the moment, or even his generation, as he was creating legend after legend, and heavy weight after heavy weight in a game that turned over one-hit-wonders by the quarter. With Snoop Doggy Dogg, no one could deny his historical importance to hip hop, well ahead of it even being made. For Snoop's own part, aware of the hype surrounding his highly-anticipated debut, he explained that "I feel like I'm one of the power speakers, like a Malcolm X figure now. But you know, a lot of times little white kids come up to me, and it makes me feel damn good and even better because it's the feeling of a straight ghetto man finally proving his stuff to the whole society. Sometimes I ask them if they really listen to the tape, and they know every word. I'm not prejudiced in my rap, I just kick the rhymes."

Leaving the production to Dre, Snoop went onto blow like a nuclear bomb upon the industry when his album debuted at number one in 1994, the same week he was indicted on charges of First Degree Murder in a drive-by shooting eerily similar to the gang-lifestylings Snoop reflected in his lyrics and image as a rap star. Ironically, the hype surrounding the trial only fueled record sales, but thankfully did not distract from the praise heaped on Dr. Dre for yet another G-Funk masterpiece. *Doggystyle* was filled with verbal and vocal feats that meet its three-mile-high expectations. *The Chronic's* slow, heavy beats were a sonic representation of angry depression as accurate as Cobain's feedback blasts; but *Doggystyle* was leaner, with its high-tempo Isaac Hayes- and Curtis Mayfield-derived tracks. The *Doggystyle* album was hailed by many as a masterpiece. Virtually every song on Snoop's debut was a classic.

The Source, meanwhile, would hail the album in a review as a masterpiece in which "virtually every song on Snoop's debut is a classic...Unfortunately, nobody makes music like this anymore."

The success of Doggystyle would stretch comfortably through 1994, selling over 4 million copies, and cementing the producer and his protégé their respective status as the forefathers of G-Funk. Amazingly, for the length of time its influence would span, according to Dre, "I did Doggystyle in 4 weeks."

Chapter 6. Doggystyle

As 1995 unfolded, Dre was busy but comfortable, a position that perhaps didn't suit him given the sound and times he was surrounded by. Outlining Death Row's ambitious plans for the year—even prior to Suge Knight's signing of Tupac Shakur— you'd never have known an era would be ending in the next 12 months, "right now, we've got the Dogg Pound album, *Dogg Food*, comin' out…Of course, we're workin' on a new Snoop Dogg album called *The Doggfather*, and The Lady of Rage, her new album, *Eargasms*."

Still, as busy as the producer's deck was, he seemed conscious of the fact that Death Row's run couldn't last forever, admitting that "I know this shit isn't gonna last forever, so when I decide I want to stop, I want to be ready."

Everything would change when Tupac joined Death Row's fold toward the end of 2005, a move Dre reportedly disapproved of behind the scenes. So tense was the mood in the studio, recalled engineer Tommy D, who remixed 'California

Love' with Dre for Tupac's 'All Eyez on Me' album, that he admitted later, "fuck it, I can say it (now): Dre really didn't want nothing to do with that record. He didn't like it at all that 2pac came to Death Row, which I thought was kind of interesting, 'cause I remember he said, 'That's it, I'm done with Death Row now that 2pac is here.'"

Continuing, the engineer revealed that 'California Love' was originally intended by Dre to be his first single on his 'Aftermath' label, but that Suge hi-jacked the song for Tupac's album, tactfully squeezing one last hit out of Dre for Death Row before he left. As Tommy D reasoned that "if you look at that album, he didn't do shit on 'All Eyez On Me' except for 'California Love,' which basically was, ughhh, that was going to be his single for Aftermath, right? And Suge heard that shit and said, 'Fuck it,' and rushed up to Dre's house and made him put 2pac on there. So basically, he lost his first single for Aftermath, and it ended up being the first single for 2pac because the original version of that is three verses with Dre rapping on it. The only person who's got that original version is DJ Jam, Snoop's DJ. So basically Suge was like, 'Fuck it, we're putting 2pac on that shit, and this is going to be the single off the record.'

That shit was dope. Suge ain't no dummy." Bailed out of jail by Suge Knight for $1.4 Million, the investment in Shakur would pay off handsomely for Knight, but the massive East Coast/West Coast feud he and Shakur helmed would leave Dre feeling alienated from what the label had originally sought to stand for. Shakur even went so far as to make Dre a target shortly following his departure, with the rapper claiming with conspiratorial, vague accusations that "I got Dre off Death Row…. Dre is doing his own thing, it doesn't effect us…Dre was one of my heroes in the music business. But I was like, no matter how dope he is, if you not down for one of his homeboys…Snoop brought him back, when he was just a relic, when niggas was dissin' him…then I don't wanna be a part of him or around him or nothing. Plus, I feel that what was done in the dark will come to light. There are secrets that everybody's gonna find out about."

Being the consummate professional, Dr was a team player prior to his exit from Death Row, filming a video with Tupac for the wildly popular single that drove 'All Eyez on Me' to sell 5 million copies in 2 months. Even more important though for the producer personally, it was the song that kept Dre's production relevant at a time when hip hop was very in the calm before a storm of musical transition that would come thundering down upon the industry as Death Row began to fall off in late 1996. Thankfully, Dre would make the decision to focus on music over drama and end his affiliation with Death Row in late 1995 for the sake of his career in the longer term.

Explaining the logic of his decision at the time, Dre reasoned that "I just wanted to start over clean...where whether I fail or succeed, it is on me...It stopped being fun...I saw an engineer get beat down once for rewinding the tape too far...(Plus), I don't even miss going out to parties or clubs and stuff...Whenever we want to have a function, we do our own thing, real private with just people that we know. We still turn the music up, have drinks and party, but it's a lot more comfortable...I was out of control...I was wildin' out, partying, women...I think the business and all the fame and fortune just sucked me in, and I had to step back and see I was ruining everything that I had worked so hard at building."

So sure of his decision, Dre even relinquished all rights to the masters from the music he'd created under the Death Row umbrella, a clear sign that in Dre's eyes, something needed to change, and that it was time to bring the era he had founded to a temporary close. Even if one were to term it a commercial hibernation, Dre was still alive and well in the studio plotting rap's next revolution.

Dr. Dre in the Studio

> *"Doing records with Dre is like going to school, because if you sit and you watch, and you look and you learn, the guy is teaching you how to make great records...anything you hear over there is Dr. Dre.*
>
> —*D.O.C.*

Chapter 7
The Aftermath of G-Funk is Born...

1996 and 1997 were troubled times for everyone in hip hop. The fact that Puffy became a solo rap star is the best proof of that fact. Rap needed somewhere new to go, and Dre for one was deep in creative thought in the lab figuring out just where that was. The history of Death Row's fall from grace is widely known: namely that once Dre made the decision to leave the label's fold, it was the beginning of the end. Out of Dre's exit, a feud predictably erupted between Suge Knight and the remaining members of the Death Row clique—one Dre tried to take the high road with to stay clear of. It was the same logic that had caused him to leave the label in the first place.

The hype had begun to get in the way of Dre's work in the studio, as he explained "there were fights in the studio, engineers getting beat up, just senseless things going on. It got to the point where I couldn't take it anymore. Still, it was difficult to leave. It was like a divorce...One thing I've learned, from experience and from talking to people like Quincy Jones who have been in the business a long time, is that once you get successful, everyone wants to be your friend... But a lot of those people don't have your best interests in mind. I finally had to sit down at one point a few years ago and try to picture myself 10 years from now and imagine which people I wanted around me, which people were really a positive force in my life. That list turned out to be very small. But the list of people around me at the time could have filled the Forum."

Once Dre was out on his own again, rather than rush out another solo LP before he was ready, the producer chose to release an experimental, test-the-waters kind of release with 'Dr. Dre Presents: The Aftermath.' A compilation featuring a wide variety of styles, ranging from the album's hit single, 'Been There, Done That', a Dre solo song to 'East Coast/West Coast Killer', a group single featuring New York rap stars including Nas and KRS One among others designed to demonstrate that Dre had nothing to do with the East Coast/West Coast beef his former label was presently at the height of.

In showing how desperate he had become without Dre, Suge Knight even went as far in an interview as suggesting that Dre had taken credit for music on Snoop's album he hadn't actually produced, even making the ridiculous claim that "Daz produced the second half of 'Doggystyle.'" While this assertion was laughable, a large number of credible sources came to Dre's defense anyway, beginning with D.O.C., who logically laid out the reasoning for why Knight's argument was both ludicrous and fundamentally flawed, and in the end of any examination, outright laughable, commenting that "you can print this so your people will understand...Let me explain something to you...What Dr. Dre gives those young men, they can't give you enough money for, what that guy

Chapter 7. The Aftermath of G-Funk is Born...

gives these young producers that are trying to come up. The only reason Dre even has anybody else in there fucking with him is because he's lazy. That's the only reason when Dre is in the studio, that shit is coming out of his mind and none of these other guys are responsible for it and I was there from day 1, 'till fuckin' '94 or '95."

Continuing, D.O.C. explained that "doing records with Dre is like going to school, because if you sit and you watch, and you look and you learn, the guy is teaching you how to make great records… Anything you hear over there is Dr. Dre. Even if Dr. Dre left the studio and allowed those guys to make their own records, part of that shit would still be Dr. Dre and believe me that's only the good part. These guys know nothing about making great beats and have very little idea about making a great song and wouldn't know a hit if you took 'Thriller' before it came out and smacked them with it."

Daz for his own part made no effort to back up Suge's claims, instead readily crediting Dre as a primary influence on his own production style, framing the Dr. as more a mentor than anything else, explaining that "Warren G taught me how to use the drum machine, then I took what I learned on the drum machine to Dr Dre to learn all that other special stuff…Dr Dre and Warren G played a big part of my career. Working the drum machine, then how to put it down on tape."

Longtime Dre collaborator at Aftermath, Mel Man, in later years came vigorously to Dre's defense at the aforementioned accusation, explaining that "Dre does not steal credit from others. In my experience with Dre, I have ALWAYS gotten proper credit and full publishing. Since the first Aftermath album Dre has given proper credit to every songwriter, producer, musician, engineer, whoever. Dre told me he learned how not to run a label during his Death Row days. He vowed to give proper credit to everyone who works on each track. Whether Dre produces or co-produces, Dre's name will almost always go first. That's just the way it is. The only time it doesn't is when Dre doesn't actively work on the making of the track. If it is finished and he jumps on and adds or changes he will not be the first name. But if Dre is active in the true creation of the track he will go first, and rightfully so as Dre is the orchestrator and director of every track. At Death Row, Dre and every other artist I talked to has told me Suge would let Dre get his own publishing but Suge would basically steal everyone else's. In music, getting publishing credit is almost everything. Whether Snoop or Kurupt or whoever wrote the verse it didn't matter. Suge publishing would get the credit...Dre was the mastermind behind the production of the tracks (of Doggy Style and the Chronic). Obviously I wasn't there during the Death Row days but everyone I have talked to during my time with Dre who was actually there said that Dre was the main force, the main producer and orchestrator of every track...In the end though Suge would not pay them correctly so a lot of people left. Suge stole credits and publishing from the musicians and writers all the time. And although Dre couldn't (although maybe he should have) force Suge to change as co-owner of Death Row, he was ultimately responsible, and Dre felt really bad about it. He felt responsible although it wasn't really his fault. That was a major factor in starting Aftermath. Dre

Chapter 7. The Aftermath of G-Funk is Born...

wanted to run a label the correct way and make sure everyone who worked with him got full credit and the correct publishing. I can honestly say Dre has never cheated me or anyone else I know during my time at Aftermath...If you ask anyone who has ever worked with Dre if he treats them fairly they will all say yes. If you are willing to put in the work it takes to be successful Dre will treat you and compensate you like family. He will reward you for your efforts...Hopefully this sheds a little light on things. Dre is far from perfect, even very irritable sometimes, but in this business of music you will find few people as giving and humble as Dr. Dre."

Once Suge Knight was in jail, Tupac was dead, and Snoop was contemplating his own exit from the label, it was clear that the first era of G-Funk had come to an end. Interscope had immediately signed Dre to a $10 Million dollar label deal out of which Aftermath Entertainment was born. While it would go onto become the most powerful independent hip hop label as the new millennium unfolded, Dre was in no hurry as he knew he had time on his side. The first thing clear to anyone was that a new generation of stars would be required to launch the next generation of hip hop, and of course, Dre was secretly plotting away in the studio as 1997 began with hip hop's next single revolutionary, Eminem. Ushering in a new cast of stars for hip hop's next revolution also meant enlisting a behind-the-scenes team of collaborators that would assist Dre in sculpting the next sonic generation of rap. This began with Mike Elizondo, who began working with Dre in 1997, explaining that the two first met "in 1997 through an engineer named Segal, who I knew from high school. Dre was looking for new blood and wanted to use live musicians, which was rare at the time. He didn't want to risk someone else sampling the same song as him; he wanted something unique... At first, I would go in on bass, with a guitarist, keyboardist, and Dre on his drum machine...Later, there were some sessions where the other musicians were booked for other sessions, so I'd play bass, guitar, and keyboard. I started bringing in guitars and pedals and keyboards that Dre hadn't heard, and that enabled me to carve a niche as a multi-instrumentalist/writer. Eventually, Dre and I developed a shared musical vocabulary; I'd know what he wanted without him having to say much."

Finding a kindred musical spirit with Elizondo, the engineer formed a partnership with Dre that would last for the next decade, and the early product of which would produce much of the material that established hip hop's next generation and evolution of sound between 1999 and 2002. As Elizondo explained, "we created tracks that became songs on Dre's 2001 CD and Eminem's first two discs...The first song (I co-wrote) that came out was 'The Real Slim Shady'...I initially played a bass line on the song, and Dre, Tommy Coster Jr. and I built the track from there. Em (Eminem) then heard the track, and he wrote the rap to it...Having a hit

Chapter 7. The Aftermath of G-Funk is Born...

song on the radio definitely changed my world, in terms of being in the music business…But I really didn't have time to think about the success. I was busy in the studio working with Dre on several other, artist projects. We started working with Eve, Mary J. Blige and Xzibit." Prior to hooking up with Elizondo, Dre had still been finding his footing throughout the remainder of 2006 with the release of 'The Firm', a group album featuring AZ, Foxy Brown, Nas and Dre. The record, like its predecessor 'Dr. Dre Presents: The Aftermath' went gold, but failed to translate into the prior sales standard of platinum status Dre had experienced with virtually every project he'd helmed from the decade prior. From Dre's point of view, he was just sampling the times, arguing that "people in hip-hop don't understand that when someone had a bad year, it doesn't automatically mean they're finished in the game…After The Firm project people were saying that I fell off. Everybody was expecting a classic record, but it's difficult to make a classic every year."

Dr. Dre in the Studio

"That's Dre's approach: a hypnotic core groove beneath the vocals, with subliminal changes coming in and out, that keeps on cycling."

—*Mike Elizondo, longtime Dr. Dre collaborator on the essence of the producer's production style.*

Chapter 8
1997 – 1999

The time that spanned between 1997 and 1999 provides us with our most in-depth study of Dr. Dre in the studio, since the producer was virtually locked away, working with a variety of new creative blood on a plethora of tracks that would come to define hip hop from 1999 on into the first half of the millennium.

With the advent of Protools and digital recording, Dre was also adapting to the implied advancements in technology and how they naturally altered the recording and producing process from the years Dre had produced on reel-to-reel analog tape. Joking at the time that "I'm actually still learning with all the new technology," Dre seemed to have found a truly new creative lease on life. Describing the creative process behind the Midas touch he'd developed to producing over the past decade in the game, Dre explained that "I don't have a main instrument. I feel my brain is my instrument. In my opinion, I'm not really that good of a musician. That's why I hire the best musicians around. Like Camara Kambon, he's one of the keyboard players, and Mike and Scott. Everybody just adds their part to the soup and it comes together."

Dre's collaborate process in the creation of songs still allowed him plenty of room to coach his team, but in the same time, he was in the unique position to be running the equivalent of an Ivy League Hip Hop College, wherein Dre was not only discovering the next generation of trend-setting rap producers, but also by turning protégé after protégé out of Aftermath, cementing his influence derivatively over generation after generation to come of hip hop.

Dre's production team at Aftermath included his engineers Maurico 'Veto' Iragorri, who described his essential role as one in which "Dre wants me to make his stuff sound as clean and clear as possible. I always EQ the tape. We put a lot of bottom on kicks, even snares, and get it set so, when it comes back, it already sounds EQ'd. (Dre) expects me to make the session run smoothly—have everything set up and ready to go when he walks in…The other thing he depends on me for is to know everything we've done and where it's cataloged on DAT. If he plays a beat that we did for Mary J. Blige, I have to know which one he's talking about and play it for him right there. Of course, I know where it's at because I recorded it."

Another member of Dre's team, Larry 'Uncle' Chapman, was Aftermath's all-around production manager, wherein, according to Chapman, "Dre comes up with the ideas and I've got to put it all together. Basically, he makes one call to me and I do the rest."

The creative core of Dre's team consisted of Mike Elizondo and Scott Storch, both of whom would go in the millennium to become A-list producers in their own right. According to Elizondo, a typical session would unfold where "Dre, Scott, and myself will show up at the studio and just start vibing. Dre will have some beats going and I'll start with a guitar riff or a bass line—we start jamming. Once an idea sounds good, the skeleton of it, Dre will ask Veto to start rolling the DAT. While Dre and the artist are writing the lyrics, we'll be laying the track down on two-inch. That's the beginning stage of it...On Snoop's The Last Meal record, it was just Dre and I goofing around. I started off with the guitar riff and he'd have the drums and there would be something there that would spark an idea. Then we would start building on top of that. My big thing is—in any situation—to just try and latch on and find a role and do that. With Dre, it began with being his musician, then it led to doing co-writes on some things, then the Snoop record, with some co-production...We have a routine for writing and recording. We would show up at the studio at 3:00 pm, almost like a day job. Then Dre would usually throw up some drum beats, and then we'd fire up the keyboards and G5 (Apple) computer. I would play keyboards and guitars. Sometimes we would work with other writers, such as Scott Storch, Mark Batson and Che Pope. We would find sounds that meshed with Dre's grooves."

Elaborating, Scott Storch adds that "there's no one particular formula. I get cracking on a couple of beats with Mike and Mel-Man—we try to come up with the best music collectively. But, typically, Dre will come in with a beat idea and then we all play around it." Dre elaborated on Elizondo's description of his recording routine, explaining that "I use the same engineer every day. I work with the same player or players every day. Once I find something that's working for me, and I dig it, that's it. I work with a player named Mike Elizondo, it's usually just me and him. He's a bassist, and he's learning keys and guitar right now. So it's pretty much just me, him, and my engineer Veto (Mauricio Iragorri) in the studio every day just grinding out the tracks; we just go. Every day I come in the studio I try to lay at least two or three tracks down, at least that, before we start working on vocals."

Dr. Dre in the Studio

One of Dre's greatest strengths as a producer—specifically the area of coaching performances out of musicians—was the essence of his creative process as a producer by that point; preferring original compositions for the most part over sampling, which had been a bedrock of his production style during the latter 1980s and the first half of the 1990s. The one difference was the fact that Dre re-recorded the majority of the samples he used with live musicians, so the decision post-leaving Death Row to continue with the live music formula, but change the nature of the sessions from re-creation to creation in the first place was remarkable at the time. By Dre's logic, samples were becoming too expensive to clear, due in part to the boon of publishing revenue that had come in over the past six years out of production imitations of the G-Funk sound Dre had founded. Explaining Dre's mastery of the art of writing in the studio—a thing many producers in genres outside of hip hop had stayed away from altogether, but which is much within the world of rap production as songs are created and constructed in an entirely unique process to traditional band recording—Mike Elizondo explained that "Dre has incredible ears, both rhythmically and harmonically. He knows if something is off and he'll sing a note he wants to hear, and that one little change will make the part happen. He's a great producer who knows how to pick the right combination of people to come in and create. Dre is also an encyclopedia of music. He's hip to the Beatles, hard rock, classical music, jazz, funk, and R&B. So if I come up with a psychedelic Mellotron part over his beat, he can easily identify it and appreciate it. The whole hip-hop culture is based on a DJ mentality; these folks are record enthusiasts. Dre didn't learn how to play piano—he learned how to spin vinyl records and move a crowd at a party…you can't look at it the same way you look at traditional songwriting, where there's an intro, verse, pre-chorus, chorus, bridge, and so on. You have to know where the music came from: people working turntables at parties, trying to find a hypnotic beat that would keep everyone on the dance floor...The key is that's Dre's approach: a hypnotic core groove beneath the vocals, with subliminal changes coming in and out, that keeps on cycling. That suits me well, because I've always been content to play something simple and not draw attention to what I'm doing. I like being the band's sort of subliminal force. I always try to play as little as possible to get the job done; I think it's best to be asked to step out, as opposed to coming across too busy and being told to tone it down. It's a real challenge to create a repetitive piece of music that will appeal to the average person at a club or vibing out at home, without getting boring."

Another of Dre's close collaborators during this period was Scott Storch, a fledgling producer and keyboard player for the ROOTs. Describing the genesis of the duo's, Storch explains that his collaboration on Dre's comeback hit, 'Still Dre', also helped in the same time to give him his first big break in the spotlight from a production side, such that "as the years passed and my reputation grew as the talented keyboardist in America's premier live hip-hop 'band,' (The Roots) I began extending my reach, taking on production opportunities. Then my big break came when my keyboard riff laced the mammoth lead single to Dr. Dre's comeback album, 'Still D.R.E.' Working alongside Dre obviously had its pluses, and soon I found myself co-producing the lead single to Xzibit's Restless album, 'X,' and getting the opportunity to produce three tracks for Snoop Dogg's Tha Last Meal...I have to say about the Dr.... he's shown me a lot of things that will help me go a long way and hopefully one day I'll reach his status...The only person I'd say I have (an allegiance) to is Dr. Dre. As far as he's concerned, he wants me to make as much money as I can...Dr. Dre and I have been working together since the chronic, and it's just like you work hard for a camp and there's loyalty there sometimes, and Dre has definitely proven to be a loyal person, and he knew I was capable of making some records, so he put me in the studio with 50 and we had a little success, so he ran ultimately the record they felt was the best record on the album as the singles, he had the vision and the faith in what I do and obviously what 50 did on the records and there it is…Dre opened the door for me, and just having my name mentioned next to his raised my stock…Doors that were once closed to me were swinging wide open."

With Dre's discovery of the greatest overnight phenomenon since Snoop Doggy Dogg—this time in the form of the great white hope, Eminem—the doors would soon come screaming off the hinges as Dre ushered in the next generation of hip hop's coming future in late 1997 when he signed the unknown Detroit genius. Eminem would gain overnight status as one of the top 10 greatest lyrical emcees of all time, both based on his lyrical content and his multi-styled delivery that didn't just raise the bar on existing styles of rapping, but invented new ones entirely. The two would quickly establish a constantly-reciprocating creative relationship that worked to produce a level of success both that had never been witnessed in hip hop up to that point. Of course, in the context of Dre, this was not that uncommon an occurrence to witness. With Eminem however, Dr. Dre would raise the bar above and beyond the industry's widest expectations—commercially, culturally, and creatively.

Dr. Dre said on spotting new talent "It's just a feeling that I get. It's a look that I look for. It's the way that they carry themselves. Of course, the talent has to be there. I look for somebody that when you hear their voice, you know it's them right off the top; it's no question. And we have to be able to get along. The talent gets you in the door; the personality keeps you there. I have to feel like I can work with somebody that I wouldn't mind leaving the studio and going to have dinner with and just chopping it up. That has nothing less than that."

DR. DRE... "Hot Pics"

Dr. Dre in the Studio

Dr. Dre and his wife of 10 years, Nicole Young, wih whom he has 3 children.

Dre with Snoop and Quincy Jones at the Vibe Awards.

. DR. DRE... *"Hot Pics"*

Dre, Snoop, Ice Cube, and Eminem on the 2000 "Up in Smoke" Tour, one of the top 10 grossing tours of the year, capitalizing on the 5X platinum comeback success of Dre's "The Chronic 2001" LP.

Dr. Dre and Snoop Dogg gracing the cover of Rolling Stone Magazine at the height of the Chronic's success in 1993, profiling the launch of the G-Funk revolution, and Snoop Dogg as Dre's next great discovery and hip hop's first rapper with Rock Star status.

69

Dr. Dre in the Studio

Dre protege 50 Cent with his G-Unit Crew of platinum selling rap stars Lloyd Banks and Young Buck.

The Dream Team: Eminem, 50 Cent, and Dr. Dre at the MTV Music Awards in 2003.

. DR. DRE… *"Hot Pics"*

Dr. Dre accepting one of his many production awards in 2001.

Dr. Dre in the Studio

> "Eminem crashed the mainstream in the late '90s, creating a storm of controversy and record-breaking sales not seen since Snoop Dogg's debut. With super-producer Dr. Dre behind the boards, Eminem scored mega-hits."
>
> —*Rolling Stone Magazine*

Chapter 9
Eminem

There is no one—or one million—ways to editorialize Eminem where the full scope of his permanent impact on hip hop could be summarized, or even captured. Phenomenon is even shallow in terms of the depth of the impression he left on his fans, critics and arch enemies. America's first true hip hop antagonist, Eminem broke past the stereotypes because his listening audience, the one Dr. Dre had discovered with N.W.A.'s breakout 'Straight Outta Compton' a decade earlier, was now being properly translated from a lyrical vantage point in context of relevance to rap's biggest single listening demographic—angry white males. Eminem gave them a voice for the first time, much in the way rap stars had for the young, black male in the 1980s.

Moreover, this message was delivered over an already extremely familiar musical soundscape in the context of Dre's production, making it feel that much more natural to embrace Eminem's music. The biggest prop Dre could get as a producer was not even for the music he created with the rapper, but rather the fact that he proved himself again a great A&R man, the true bread and butter of the record business— in terms of breaking new talent. Dre had a track record to build upon with D.O.C., Ice Cube, N.W.A., and Snoop Doggy Dogg; but with Eminem, he would outpace his past records at a pace that even took Dre by surprise at the time it first happened.

Music and cultural historians will be studying the impact of Eminem's influence over hip hop for decades upon decades to come. Along with any investigation into what made him lyrically so profound, those academics will equally have to examine the wildly kindred creative interplay between Eminem and Dr. Dre during the duration of the collaboration.

It was the next revolution of rap, and in truth, Eminem in essence had his own generation in hip hop. He had no competitors or viable rivals, and his production was the top of the game even before he'd reached it. Moreover, because the translation of Eminem's musical message was so instant, few noticed Dre had been gone at all even as his latest protégé was appearing for the first time.

Because Eminem spoke for so many millions of working and middle class white kids—ALL of whom had grown up listening to Dre via the Death Row era between 1991 and 1997—the arrival of Eminem and Dr. Dre worked to make rap exciting again because they gave the fans something truly new. The duo pushed rap in a new direction whose evolution VH1 described as one in which "producer/performer Dr. Dre changed the rap game twice: First with NWA's groundbreaking 1988 debut *Straight Outta Compton*, and again with his own disc, 1992's *The Chronic*. After teaming up with Eminem in 1999, he once again made a mammoth move, putting skeletal but compelling backdrops on the rhymer's incendiary diatribes to created *The Slim Shady LP*."

Chapter 9. Eminem

Rap fans had bought into Eminem so quickly because of his talent no doubt, but what put him over the top was the 'Dre protégé' sticker, which gave the white rapper a stamp of endorsement in the credibility department that would have otherwise taken years to earn. Fans wanted to believe that Dre had magically discovered Eminem's demo, but in reality, while the 'Dre discovered Em' twist was spun by Interscope publicists, it was Interscope CEO Jimmy Iovine who had first suggested to Dre that he take Eminem on as an artist, knowing the rapper's affiliation with Aftermath would go farther in cementing his authenticity to hip hop fans than if he had been merely introduced through Interscope, who were viewed as a corporate, mainstream conglomerate.

Recalling how quickly Dre knew for his own part that the pair were a creative fit, he explained that "I was at (Interscope chairman) Jimmy Iovine's house one night. Usually when I'm over there, we listen to demos in his garage. We finished listening to everything that we had been working on that night and he said, 'I want you to check this out. What do you think about this kid?' Jimmy pops in the cassette. I was blown away…(with) his lyrical content. He sounded like he had big-ass balls. He finds ways to rhyme words that don't seem like they should rhyme. I felt that…I knew I had to work with him right then. I met him about two days after that and the next day we were in the studio at my house.

We came up with four joints that night and three of them made it onto his first album…We did a lot of Eminem's first record at my home studio. Actually the first song we did together, 'My Name Is,' was done there." Realizing the opportunity he had on his hands to further push the boundaries of hip hop that N.W.A. had first expanded in the late 1980s, Dre felt he had an opportunity to make history all over again in working with Eminem, explaining that "I didn't even know he was white when I heard the demo. Jimmy Iovine told me a little later. Then my wheels started turning.

I thought he would be able to get away with saying a lot more than I would get away with saying. If a black guy said that stuff, people would turn the radio off. That's reality." The duo's first collaboration, over the course of 'The Slim Shady LP', would produce two hit singles, including Dre's first since 'Been There, Done That' over two years earlier, with 'My Name Is' and 'Guilty Conscience.'

Debuting at number one, and going onto sell 5 million copies, Eminem's first album became a instant soundtrack for a generation. Where fans had taken immediately to the lyrical trade-offs and interplay between Dre and Snoop Dogg years before, with Eminem, Dre had an opportunity to reinvent and re-introduce himself freshly to hip hop listeners. In the process, he was creating a waiting list of sorts for his own pending comeback LP, 'The Chronic 2001.'

Eminem's overnight success reinvented Dre in the process, and the duo became the most cutting-edge thing on the radio and video waves. Moreover, the success of Eminem's debut, 'The Slim Shady LP' served to establish Aftermath's credibility as a label much in the way 'The Chronic' had for Death Row in 1992.

For the first time, Dre was successfully in control of his own destiny, and his success proved any naysayers wrong about his chances without Death Row for success. Dre had multiple platforms now from which to spread his influence out about hip hop at large—employing a three-prong advantage included his label using the success of Eminem as an opportunity to attract the crème of hip hop's up and coming crop, namely with the signing of Eminem, and then with 50 Cent as the millennium unfolded.

Chapter 9. Eminem

Critically, Eminem scared the shit out of white America far more than the young, black male stereotype ever had. Eminem had plenty of hype to justify. He was not only the first new protégé from Dr. Dre in years, he was the first new sound from Dr. Dre in years. He was also a white MC in a rap scene that hadn't gotten any less black in two decades... Eminem had to bring something new to the table, and he did with *The Slim Shady* LP... The beats on *Slim Shady* were low-affect West Coast funk in the Dre style, with the Doctor producing… But the steady midtempo grooves didn't distract anyone from the voice.

Eminem has skills—he's a warp-speed human rhyming dictionary with LL Cool J's gift for the killer dis. He doesn't rap about the hustling high life, just minimum-wage jobs, high school beat-downs and decidedly ill drug dementia. As a hip-hop disciple inheriting a twisted American racial history he didn't create, Eminem…speaks for a lot of his fans.

At the time of his first album release in the summer of 1999, Dre more than anyone knew Eminem was still on the outskirt of his own true commercial potential, commenting that "Eminem… pays attention to what he's doing in the studio, and he makes sure his records are coming out right…I wasn't worried that people would react against him because he's white. The hardest thugs I know think this white boy's tight…He…has a strong career ahead of him…I knew it was going to be big. I didn't know it was going to be this big. I didn't know it was going to be half this big. I knew people were going to get into him, and love him, and just think he's a crazy ass white boy."

Delving into the pair's creative process in the studio, Dre explained that "there's no big scientific explanation. We don't wake up at two in the morning, call each other, and say, 'I have an idea. We gotta get to the studio.' We just wait and see what happens when we get there."

For Eminem's part, while he may have been living in the creative moment with Dre while the pair was recording, he was taking quiet from the jump on Dre's production style, explaining some of the progress he made as a result of working with Dre as a recording artist a process in which "Dre showed me how to do things with my voice that I didn't know I could do…The way to deliver rhymes and (shit). I'd do something I thought was pretty good, and he'd say, 'I think you can do it better.' So we did it again and again, and he was right…Trying to rap over a Dre beat for the first time did something for me…I didn't know how to work a drum machine; I didn't know the first thing about it. I was making raps to other people's songs. It would be distracting. I remember especially writing a lot to Nas' first album. I had no equipment and didn't know what to do. Between Infinite and The Slim Shady LP, Denaun (Porter of D12) was making all those beats. When I got with Dre, it was all about rhymes, rhymes, rhymes…I didn't know how to write choruses back then. My man DJ Butta would scratch in choruses from other records. I always had melodies in my head, and then I started getting better at writing hooks and was like, 'This is easy.' I realized the hook is just summing up the whole song or what point you're trying to get across."

While Eminem found himself growing as an emcee through the early stages of his collaboration with Dr. Dre, he also caught the bug as a student of Dre's producing style, such that the more I got in the studio with Dre, the more I started picking up and watching what he was doing. My first experience making beats is my first album. The first drum pattern I ever made was to (singing) 'I never meant to give you mushrooms girl.' I already had the melody in my head from the night before. I didn't know how to work the metronome, but if you put the click on for me, I knew how to make a drum pattern. Then I was like, 'Yo, I know how to do this!' After that, I did the drum pattern to 'Still Don't Give a Fuck.' I'd go to Dre and hum the melody, and he was like, 'You don't even realize it, but you're producing.' But I had no idea."

Validating Eminem's interest in the production side of the recording craft, Dre explains that "it's a perfect example of an artist coming in and taking advantage of the situation. That's what he did, he came in, and he works his ass off. Everybody that came in the studio and really put their thing down, and really put it together has been successful with me."

Building off the wild success of 'The Slim Shady LP', when Dre and Eminem began working on his follow-up LP in late 1999, it was business as usual for Dre in terms of his formula for banging out hits in the moment, with the exception of 'Kill You', wherein the producer recalled that "the only time we didn't actually sit in a studio and create something on the spot was with 'Kill You.' I was talking to Em on the phone. He heard the track playing in the background and was like, 'What's that? Send me that track!' So I sent it to him, he wrote the lyrics, came down and we got busy with it."

The sophistication of the production on the 'Marshall Mathers LP', coupled with the fact that the musical mood of the album felt completely natural as a backdrop to Eminem's dark lyrical disposition throughout the majority of the record, raised the bar for both even more than 'The Slim Shady LP' had.

Discussing some of the tracks, which impressed him most from Eminem's sophomore LP, Dre recalled that "I thought 'Stan' was the best song that he's ever done. It's weird listening to that. He's in character and talking about himself. It was a brilliant record: Put together really well—the whole nine… (When I first heard 'Kim'), my jaw hit the ground. I played the song over and over about 10 times. That's one of my favorites next to 'Stan.' Just because of the aggression that he put into it. I thought it was gonna push some buttons and make people's skin crawl. It's important to get a reaction and jerk some kind of emotion out of people when they listen to what you're doing…We thought the album was done, but we didn't feel like there was anything commercial enough to put out as a first single. Once people heard the album and got into it, I knew we had a second and third single. But we needed that big opener. So me and Em came back in the studio for about a week or so, and created 'The Real Slim Shady.' Boom! We felt it right away. It was one of those moments. He had the hook already. We put music to that, and it came out right. My kids were singing it, you know what I'm saying? That was enough for me."

Eminem appeared rightfully excited about the expanded number of tracks Dre would produce on the rapper's highly-anticipated sophomore LP, explaining that "(Dre's) doing a lot more than he was. He did three tracks on the last album. He's got at least seven on this one and we ain't even finished the work we're doing. Dre has been so busy with his own album. He's been mixing it down and shit, but as soon as he's finished, we're gonna start getting in there and knocking shit out like we did the last one."

Eminem, in recalling that in context of his development as a producer, offered a unique glimpse into his and Dre's specific process for creating a song, such that "the first record I ever produced while Dre was in the room was 'The Way I Am.' I had a piano loop in my head and I didn't want to forget it, so I recorded on a little handheld recorder. And the whole flight to L.A., I had it in my head and wrote the lyrics. I didn't even have a drum beat in my head. So when I got there, I asked his keyboard player to play the lick. Then I had to figure out how the beat would go, so I picked out the drums I wanted and asked Dre to turn the click on. So I started making a pattern using Dre's sounds and it was like night and day from anything we had ever produced. After that I did the drum pattern for 'Criminal,' 'Renegade,' and 'Cleaning Out My Closet.' That's when I really got into drums sounds." One credible source observing Eminem's development as a follow up-and-coming producer out of the Aftermath stable was

Scott Storch, who commented in regards to Eminem's production skills that "Em is a very talented individual. The way he does things in the studio and how quickly he learns is amazing. People say that his music sounds the same or whatever but anybody can make a beat, the thing they need to realize is you need to create a signature beat so that every time you hear a beat you automatically think 'yeah Lil Jon or Dr Dre or just Blaze.'"

As for Mike Elizondo's observations regarding Eminem's development as a producer under Dre's tutelage, he described an evolution in which "Em is very prolific…(When we were working on the Eminem Show'), it was like the old Motown style of working, with a group of us creating the music and tracks in the same room…(I work) very closely (with Em); I'm in the studio with (him) all the time. Those guys are very musical, more so than people probably realize. They'll come in with an idea for a bass or keyboard line and hum it to us. Eminem has interacted with me on bass, guitar, and keyboard…I'm one of the fortunate few who gets to see how deeply these artists are involved in their tracks. They spend hours and hours in the studio working on their craft."

While Eminem was locked away working on his third LP with Dr. Dre, 'The Eminem Show', he was also following Dre's lead in the A&R aspect of producing, signing New York's hottest rapper 50 Cent to a $1 Million record deal in 2002, cementing his own status as mogul-on-the-rise. Of course, it was implied that Dre would helm some of the production on what would become the best selling rap album of 2003, 'Get Rich or Die Tryin.'

By encouraging his artists and co-producers to spread their wings, Dre was in the process of raising his own bar of credibility, relevance, and visibility among an entire new breed of hip hop listener. By signing 50 Cent to Aftermath, under a

Chapter 9. Eminem

shared deal with Eminem's 'Shady Records', Dr. Dre was also proving that his music was credibly Universal to both the East and West Coast, rather than merely being known as a West Coast producer, as he'd been pigeon-holed for the first half of his career.

In observing this plotting on Dre's part to expand the influence of his sound beyond what had traditionally been his home turf of G-Funk and artists who represented that culture and sound, Dr. Dre's DJ, DJ Jam, reasoned that "Dr. Dre is a kind of person (whose) he's done that all. He's tryin to look out for some other artists from different areas. He wants to make a big impression on the East coast also. He wants to make a big impression, if he can, down South. He's like the master, you know whatta mean? Dre can put it together and make it possible. So right now, he believes in what he's hearing. Look at 50 Cent, you know. He talked to Eminem and said, 'Let's do this project.' 'cause Dre knows, he knows talent, when he hear it and what can happen to, you know.

Timing is everything in the music industry. It's not about where you come from, it's where you are at the time."

This was definitely Dre's time, and building on the credibility he'd re-established among hip hop listeners with Eminem, in the fall of 2000, Dre was preparing to drop his long-awaited follow-up to 'The Chronic'.

"The Chronic 2001. The album proved that Dre's already incredible talents were getting even better, with elaborate, orchestrated production perfectly balancing funkiness and complexity."

—*Rolling Stone Magazine*

Chapter 10
The Chronic 2001

It was between 1998 and 2000 that Dr. Dre's aftermath from Death Row truly began to flourish, the impact of his first generation of hip hop beginning to gain historical recognition in a legacy context, and his relevance more applicable to the genre commercially as the millennium unfolded and hip hop's next direction commanded a leader.

Dre was experiencing something of a production renaissance, having established enough foundationally on his own as a producer to begin collaborating with other, up and coming and established producers like Mel Man, Scott Storch, Mile Elizondo, and DJ Hi Tek among others on his records.

Explaining that, from his vantage point, hip hop could not survive if it didn't grow musically in new directions, Dre reasoned that "I don't think it's possible for hip-hop to grow if producers just keep copying what has already been done…I use old records as my motivation, but I try to stay away from sampling—I'm not going to base a whole album on someone else's music...Most of the album is live...I tried to stay away from samples as much as possible. There are, I think, two samples on (the record.) I wanted most of this album to come from the brain, the heart. I didn't want to just go into the studio and use what somebody else made to get paid."

With that concept in mind, Dre had been working for the past 3 years on the masterpiece he knew would have to be a phenomenal success to fully re-establish him in his own right as a top recording artist and producer simultaneously, the edge that had always kept Dre dominant over the genre, because he could influence the game from both ends.

The creative evolution of the Chronic came out of the fluid musical routine of Dr. Dre, Mike Elizondo, Scott Storch, and others getting together in the studio each day to create, wherein "we essentially have studio jam sessions, with Dre on his MPC3000, myself, producer/keyboardist Mark Batson, and producer/programmer Che Pope. Dre starts a beat, the rest of us chime in looking for a sound or melody that will be a musical hook, and then we proceed to build a skeleton track. Ninety percent of the time, I start off writing on guitar or keyboard, and then I pick up my bass—usually my Sadowsky 5 or a Vintage 4-string. Sometimes I'll play the bass part on keyboard if it's appropriate, or just because it's in hand and I have a cool sound. We have these old Electrix Repeater 4-track looping machines that aren't made anymore. They're syncable through MIDI; you can enter your in and out loop points with a foot pedal, and the loops will be perfectly synced to the other MIDI instruments. So I'll add a four-bar loop on guitar or keyboard first, and then I'll get my bass and loop that in. It enables us to hear what the full track will sound like. We spend about 20 minutes on an idea, and when we're done we put the track onto a DAT tape, and the engineer catalogs all the sounds and saves all the sequences. Later, when an artist hears our tracks and wants to record one, we recall all the sounds, throw everything onto Pro Tools, and add finishing touches, usually to the arrangement."

Continuing in his description of how the tracks that would compose the Chronic 2001 were created, Elizondo explained that "I draw from a combination of the music I've listened to and the music I've played. I listen to Dre's drum beat, and it's almost like there's already a bass line there—I can hear it in my head. I try to be lyrical, hooky, and have a great tone, all at the same time. The bass line has to be something you won't get tired of hearing for four minutes, and it needs to be as infectious as the drum beat. I've picked up a lot from Dre in learning how to create a bass part: where notes are placed, how long to hold a note, and what type of tone to get from the bass to match or contrast the kick and bring the whole 'kit' out. He opened my eyes to those kinds of concepts. Where the notes stop makes a huge difference in what the groove feels like. The key for me is to free my mind and allow myself to be open, tune into Dre's beat, and react in the moment. There are times when I come up with a part and I have no idea why I played it. Dre's beats can get so hypnotic that sometimes I'll hear the one in the wrong place. When he starts the beat up again, my part might be a quarter-note or an eighth-note off, and I'll have to refigure it to fit the phrase!...His drum machine, an Akai MPC3000, allows you to adjust how much a pattern swings by setting a percentage. Once I heard that, it kind of re-opened my mind to all those areas in between straight and swung feels, and how many different ways there are to play eighth—and 16th-notes. Plus, you realize how you can play straight against a swung figure, or vice versa, to create tension. It's a matter of experimenting."

Other musicians and producers who collaborated with Dre during this period on material for the Chronic 2001 and related Aftermath material included one up and coming engineer/producer, Mel Man, who Dre clicked so well with he made him co-producer on The Chronic 2001. Mel Man explained the Dr.'s collaborative formula as one in which "Dre has discovered and/or used some incredible musicians during his career—Colin Wolfe, Mike Simms, Sean Thomas, T green, Scott Storch, Camara Kamron—to name a few. Dre gives all of the musicians he has used a lot of credit for being a big part of his success…While (Dre has) sampled, or replayed and expanded like (he) did in the Ruthless and Death Row years…Dre (tries)…to create MUSIC using mostly live instrumentations…(He has) used actual live drums on a number of records, as well as live bass of all types, pianos, keys, horns, guitars, flutes, sax, xylophone, etc…The fact is that Dre and Quik are the top producers in rap MUSIC because they create music and hire some incredible musicians to help them bring their ideas to musical life."

Continuing, Mel Man described some of Dre's greatest attributes as a producer and a teacher in the studio, explaining that "being a PRODUCER is so much more than being a musician. Only in rap is a producer expected to play instruments on tracks. Most music producers don't play anything on the records. Great producers do however have the 'ear' and understand melodies, and how best to maximize an instrument and the musician's potential. Dre has one of the best ears there is. Believe me, he has made me a better musician than I ever thought I could be because he knows exactly how to tweak what I play from good to great. Producers coach, discover talent, mentor, shape, mold, compose, create, adjust, innovate, arrange, focus, orchestrate, direct and so much more. Dre does all of that, and as a total package does that as well as or better than any producer in modern music history…Dre has changed his music and the sound of music itself more than once. With NWA and being the main creative force behind Ruthless records he helped change the sound of rap music and what could be said on records. With The Chronic he was the leader in bringing a fresh sound—g-funk—to music. If you bought that album when it came out in December '92 it blew you away as it was unlike anything you had ever heard before. The chronic also brought gangsta rap to the masses and made it a cultural phenomenon (along with saving Interscope from folding). When Dre left to start Aftermath he changed the course of music forever (again) with the discovery of Eminem… Dre has discovered some of the biggest artists in music history and as a producer he molded those artists by taking them from unpolished diamonds to polished multi-platinum selling artists."

Continuing his praising testimony on his teacher's behalf, Mel Man explained that, during a given recording session, "as a producer Dre works harder than anyone else and demands more from his artists than anyone else. He mentors artists and maximizes their talent. He has the incredible ability to bring the best out of any artist and helps them to perform at incredible levels or career best levels…Jimmy Iovine calls Dre the most influential record producer in music history. While I won't put him alone at the top he's definitely on the short list…Dre, as a PRODUCER, is as good as there has ever been. He is the Michael Jordan of Rap."

Confirming the rumor of over 100 tracks recorded for 'The Chronic 2001', Mel Man proclaimed that "Dre's vault is the stuff of legend. It is almost mythical…The vault basically has every track Dre has ever recorded. He has copies of everything he did on Death Row but can never release. You can't even imagine how many instrumentals that have accumulated over the years I've been at Aftermath. It's in the thousands. Dre keeps all his music for his own personal use and listening. He basically keeps them as a soundtrack to his life. Most of the leftovers will never be heard. Most of the unused instrumentals will never be heard, at least while Dre is alive.

There is enough music to release hundreds of albums so Dre could possibly live through music for many additional lifetimes. But you'll most likely never hear them…I have had the privilege to hear a lot of music you will never have a chance to hear and for that I am sorry. Dre usually does a great job of using the right beats and songs, but some of the unreleased music is some of the dopest shit I have ever heard. We sometimes are in awe of what Dre tosses out but Dre knows what Dre wants. Who are we to argue. We may plead and beg but in the end its Dre's music so he can do with it what he wants. I truly wish that I could let you hear the music because you are missing out on some of the most innovative and dope unreleased music in the history of this business. From Ruthless to Aftermath there are truly some great tracks out there that only Dre will ever hear…The Vault is real and does contain close to the entire Dre creative library."

Another producer who worked on the album was the legendary East Coast D.I.G.C. producer Lord Finesse, who Dre tapped to produce the most personal song to him personally. In 'The Message', Dre rapped an ode to his deceased little brother Tyree, whose death had clearly haunted the producer for years, explaining that "I was so emotional…Even now I have a hard time listening to it unless I'm alone. But for anyone who has lost a loved one, they should be able to relate."

The song appeared to offer an emotional closure of sorts, and the production process was therein that much more delicate according to Lord Finesse, who explained that "I was very flattered as a producer, coming on behalf of somebody whom one admires it is extremely gratifying. I am very lucky to have been able to work with him; he is one of the largest producers and I am almost the only one to have produced a piece for him. It is as if Quincy Jones required of me to produce it…That song was (originally going to be) on my album, and when he heard that he was like: 'Can I get that for my album?,' and who am I to tell Dr. Dre: 'No, you can't have it.'…He showed me so much love, treated me like a little brother…I would love to be a part of (the Aftermath) team, that goes without sayin', it's nothing more than being a chef in the kitchen and you get to be around a master chef that can understand who you are as a producer, from just your potential alone, as opposed to 'you've gotta have all these hit records' for someone to understand your potential, and also being a part of the Dre camp—I don't want to say Aftermath—I'm there really because of Mel-Man and Dre, it has nothing to do with Aftermath. I want to be a part of that movement because its Mel-Man and Dre and that's why I think certain conflicts came in after that, because I don't want to be an Aftermath producer, its just I want to be down with whatever they're doing as far as Mel-Man and Dre, I'm there for the cause…Being around them (in the studio), and watching and observing, and soaking in a lot of techniques and mechanics they used to produce those tracks, really I picked up a few things (from working with them.)"

Dre, for his own part, was more motivated than everyone, acknowledging at the time that "everything is riding on this album," and believing in being prepared, reportedly accumulated over 100 tracks before settling on 22 final cuts for the album. In spite of his legend, Dre seemed to take a very realistic perspective personally on why he needed the album to perform well at retail, outside the context of his professional status, with the producer explaining that "I love my lifestyle and to continue living this lifestyle, I have to continue selling records and being successful."

Conceptually, Dre explained that his ambitions for the Chronic 2001 was to take "what I did with N.W.A and 'The Chronic' and make it sound futuristic…with this record, you know what I'm saying?…We're going after the same audience, but we want to give them something fresh, an excitement that is

Dr. Dre in the Studio

missing from the hip-hop scene right now. To me, the scene is pretty much dead (artistically) There's not a lot that you hear it and you go, 'I've got to have this.'" More pointedly at his critics, Dre proclaimed that "I call Dr. Dre 2001 my shut the fuck up album, because that's what I want all these critics and haters to do — just shut up and listen to my music."

Both because he could afford it and perhaps in a nod to why he had left Death Row environmentally, Dre explained that while he'd recorded much of Eminem's debut LP at his home studio, he'd gotten rid of his home recording lab because "I kind of got tired of having a home studio because you get to the point where you want to feel like you're going to work. Plus, sometimes you have to work with people and there's just some people you don't want in your house."

In the course of creating the masterpiece that became the Chronic 2001, Dre recorded primarily out of Larrabee West, Encore, and Record One, utilizing state-of-the-art studio gear in the process that made his sound that much more advanced and cutting edge. Dre's favorite tools of the trade included the Solid State Logic Console, as well as the Studer A827. Amazingly, Dre was arguably the only hip hop producer in the game who still cut his live sessions off the floor to analog using Quantegy 499 tape, and utilized a Neve 1073 mic pre, and a Sony C800G for all vocal recording. Delving a bit into his approach and setting preferences when tracking vocals, the producer explained that "'I usually record vocals flat. The only time I put EQ on vocals when recording is if I know for a fact that I'm going to want it to sound like that during the mix…When I want a little more crispness out of the mic, I use the 1073 EQ with just a little high end. I don't use too much compression; maybe 4:1 with the outputs set to zero. I usually do my compression afterwards. I like the compressors on the SSL. I usually have the ratio up to about eight or ten on a lot of things."

Explaining his reasons sonically for preferring analog in the course of recording, Dre explained that "I tried digital a couple of times and I don't really like it. There's just something about it. For me, it's not fast enough just yet. I tried to record into Pro Tools and got one of the best Pro Tools operators down to record the music, and it's just not me. Not yet…We had the Sony 3348 in the studio, and I tried a couple of songs on it and it didn't give me the sound I wanted. The kick drum started sounding transparent. It wasn't good."

Even when mixing, Dre preferred to mix straight to DAT utilizing a Panasonic 3800, and does not like an excessive presence of outboard gear during the process, explaining that "We don't use a lot of outboard gear…I doctor the vocal as far as de-essing and maybe some low-end EQ for the kicks. We use a lot of EQ on the console and all the limiters. Most of it comes out of the SSL and into the quad compressor. I like the sound of it on the mix bus. That's the SSL quad compressor in the center of the console'. Of all the studios Dre bounced in and out of during the recording and mixing of the Chronic 2001, Dre preferred to "mix most everything at Larrabee West. I just like a studio that's comfortable, has a lot of space, and, very important, has a lounge with a kitchen…The equipment is important, but, to be honest, I'm still working on the same board I've worked on since 1990. The important part is who's pushing the buttons."

Taking just over three years to complete production on the Chronic 2001, heading into its release, Dre commented in regard to expectations for his new sound and why he took as long as he did to release the record that "people come up to me on the street and say, 'I hear something different every time I listen to your record.' That's what I like to hear…I really take a lot of time on each song and make sure it's okay—I'm my worst critic. I want to make sure it's right…It feels incredible just to be done. It feels, it feels, damn…it feels incredible, man. It's just an overwhelming experience here. I'm just happy to be out of the studio and not seeing any buttons for a while, you know."

Dre seemed particularly excited about his collaboration with Snoop Dogg, explaining that "that's the ultimate, getting back with Snoop…I think that…(is) the wisest move for me…Snoop is like my little brother…We both know that we sound best when we're together. After we got back together, it was like we had never been apart, because our chemistry is that strong. We're not afraid to give each other creative criticism, because we want to be the best we can be…It felt real good to get back with all the guys from the first 'Chronic' album. When they came in the studio, it was just like we were never apart. It was a weird feeling, like, okay, everybody just came in and grabbed pens and papers and, you know, (started) doing they thang. It was just fun. Lot of laughter, and we had fun doing the songs."

Snoop, for his part, shared Dre's enthusiasm, and feeling that their collaboration was very much a case of one hand washing the other in terms of the reciprocal benefit both artists stood to gain from reuniting. As Snoop explained, "getting back with Dre is like a dream come true, because he's the one that brought me to the light…To be able and grow and go out on my own and show him that I can do it on my own and show him why he put me in the game, and then to be able to go back to him and let him coach me a little bit more and direct me I mean, we got a lot of big plans. Me and Dr. Dre are putting together a record label right now as we speak, and so we're going to be doing a lot of big things. So that reunited thing was more than him doing three songs on my album and me doing a couple songs on his record. We're actually back together as far as being friends, the communication, supporting each other's projects and acts, and just trying to be there for each other."

Everyone involved with the project was its champion, and not only because they stood to benefit from it commercially in terms of exposure, but because working with Dre naked of all the lifestyle-related distractions that had defined life on Death Row reminded each of them why they'd signed on in the first place back in 1991 when Dre founded Death Row. More than anything else, the 'Chronic 2001' was a true piece and product of genuine genius, it innovated the way we thought about hip hop musically as listeners. It was the truest piece of hip hop perfection since the arrival of 'The Chronic' seven years and a generation earlier. Starring Eminem and Snoop Dogg on the same album only worked to reinforce that fact.

The 'Chronic 2001' wasn't merely well received, it was reveled at by the top critics in the game, celebrated by millions of hip hop fans—six million to be exact—and marveled over by industry executives. Most knew the best way to emulate the success of the Chronic was to simply follow the leader, and so Dre was once again in a position to direct hip hop's sound with almost total deference from the industry around him—i.e. things were as they should have been at that time in rap's transition out of the 1990s and into the new millennium. "There were a lot of haters out there that were saying I was washed up, I fell off, and what have you. That was probably my biggest motivation for this record".

To top off Dre's comeback, as 2001 unfolded, Dre was nominated for five Grammy Awards, and won two, including Best Rap Performance by a Duo or Group award with Eminem, and of course, Producer of the Year. The latter award was particularly validating for Dre, who explained in reflection shortly following his winning that "that was big…I love the fact that I didn't have to go on stage and give a thank you speech. I didn't have anything written down. As it turned out, when they called my name for Producer of the Year, I just stood up. That's going to be the perfect ending to my life story."

"I have definitely had a good year."

—*Dr. Dre*

Chapter 11
2000-2001

Dre used the phenomenal success of Eminem and his own 'Chronic 2001' to form a powerhouse with Aftermath, a conglomerate that embodied a distribution structure similar to that of Death Row with Interscope, but also production deals with Aftermath producers, and label deals with Aftermath artists like Eminem, whose Shady Records would release the platinum D-12 and eventually sign 50 Cent.

Naturally, Dre got a piece of everything financially, but more importantly, he could produce select tracks, which typically became singles for a variety of Aftermath artists without having to focus exclusively on any one project. Following the 3-year and 100-song epic that the recording of 'Chronic 2001' was, it was understandable that Dre wanted to avoid tying himself down, explaining that "usually it takes between nine and ten months to produce and make a record that's gonna be hot enough to present to the people."

This was made more necessary by the fact that Dre was again the most in-demand producer in the business following his 'Producer of the Year' Grammy. Examples of his strategy for keeping his sound stamped on hip hop culture was Dre's decision to spot-produce singles for any variety of artists, and to work from a supervisory position—with the exception of producing the record's radio singles—was Xhibit, whose 2000 album 'Restless', Dre executive produced, in a move that Xhibit explained as "no big decision-making process. He came to the studio and asked me if I would executive-produce his record, and I said, 'Yeah.' We started blueprinting it out, coming up with a plan of how we were going to do it."

For Dre's part in explaining his involvement in the project, he sought to make clear that it was still creatively hands-on in nature, such that "a lot people just figure that they can pay for the record, and get the title of 'executive production' when that's not the case…Executive-producing, in my mind, is helping pick the tracks, maybe producing some of the tracks, really being hands-on with the actual music: my saying, 'Xzibit, that track you got from so-and-so is not hot, let's use this track over here from so-and-so. Maybe you should rhyme about this.' Just basically helping put the record together. A lot of records have come out that have executive production credits on them, and it's just people paying for studio time—if that. Producing (on the other hand), is going into the studio and directing a record from bottom to top. My producing a record is my starting from the first hi-hat 'til the mix is done."

Xhibit, for his own part, confirmed Dre took his work equally as seriously for Xhibit's album as he had for any other, to the degree that "there is definitely a high standard when you walk into the studio...It's not as strict and straight-up as everybody thinks—it *is* a work environment, but it's relaxed and impromptu. He works with actual live musicians. You go in with more of a vibe, then once you get a direction going, you put the pieces together."

Dre also logged in production time for Busta Rhymes, Mack 10, Sticky Fingaz, and new Aftermath R&B signing 'Truth Hurts, a move which produced the hit single 'Addictave.' The singer describes the studio process with Dre as one in which "he really took it to another level...I don't get that excited over my own songs...He took another part of the Indian sample and added it to the beginning and to the middle. I can't explain it. He used another part of the sample to bring in the energy of it. It's even more club than the original. Rakim added another rhyme to the beginning, and that rhyme is hotter than the rhyme that's on the original. It's just amazing." Dre commented for his part that "(unlike Truth Hurts), I think a lot of the music the female artists are putting out right now is kind of bubble-gumish...I like it a little more edgy, closer to the type of music that I'm used to putting out...I don't feel like I know everything there is to know...If a person is hot, there's something I can learn from them. (With Truth Hurts), I learned a lot about vocal direction and just arranging vocals...I also learned that I don't see myself working with too many other female vocalists."

Dre also reunited with former Aftermath artist Eve to produce some tracks from her sophomore album on RuffRyders, 'Scorpion.' In an experience the rapper recalls as one where "(we'd) never worked closely before...I did one song (with Dre), and I am going back to L.A. to do one more. He wanted me to come up with a certain type of flow. He's really involved as far as how I flow—not so much my words, but my bounce on the track. It's great. He's very creative, and he's very excited about the project, so it's been real good energy."

Even Michael Jackson approached Dre during this time about a possible collaboration on Jackson's forthcoming album. The producer passed on the offer, explaining that "somebody approached me about working with Michael Jackson, and I did say no because I like working with new artists or people that I've worked with in the past. I can develop them from the ground up. There's no set standard that I have to live up to or anything like that. All I have to do is go in the studio, and basically they're going to bust their ass to come in there and do their thing the way it's supposed to be done."

Predictably, Dre did collaborate with Eminem over the course of 2001, this time in preparation for the rapper's third album, 'The Eminem Show', wherein, according to Dre, "his album is crazy. I mean, what more can I say? It's Eminem to the fullest," Dre said Wednesday at his Burbank, California, recording studio. "Everybody that digs the first two albums is gonna love this one...I do feel he has matured as a lyricist, but I don't know if (saying he's) moving in a different direction is accurate...His stuff is really crazy to me because just when you think, 'OK, he has run out of stuff to say, he can get no crazier than this,' something comes out of his face that gives you chills or something. Makes the hair crawl on your skin. So I think the shock value of Eminem is definitely gonna still be there, but it's just getting better...His production skills are getting really nice...I think there is one song that has Nate Dogg on it, but most of the album is just him. He's singing a lot. He's singing and doing a lot of his own choruses and harmonies. The whole nine yards."

Another strategic move Dre made was to strip his Aftermath roster down to its bare essentials again, explaining that "I actually cleared the roster to start over and regroup, because I wasn't feeling the way it was going in the beginning of Aftermath, so I think we're on the right road right now."

That meant, of course, keeping Eminem as his marquee artist, but also making a move to sign historically arguably among the top two or three greatest lyric-smiths in the game, the legendary Rakim. Dr. Dre—in spite of his own legend—was still in awe of working with the legendary emcee, so much so that, according to the producer "the first few joints we did, I had to get over the fact that I was working with Rakim...It was a little hard to direct him, you know what I mean? But now that we've been talking and getting to know each other a little bit, it's getting a little easier. I can throw some concepts at him and we can vibe...I've got to feel like I can leave the studio with you and we can go sit down and eat and enjoy each other without getting on each other's nerves...I told him I wanted it to be both of our best albums...With any project that I get involved in, I feel like there's pressure. I think that's what makes my music come out so good. I'm my worst critic, so I guess I give myself most of the pressure. More pressure than probably the public does, you know. So I just have to please myself, and once I do that usually the public digs it...When I work with a person, it's not strictly about the talent."

Unfortunately, Dre's collaboration with Rakim would not last even one full-length album, as, according to Rakim, "we had creative differences…Dre wanted to go one direction, I wanted to go another direction…For a while (we were) trying to please both sides of the fences. Later on (we decided) it was best I went my way and let him finish doing what he do, but it's still love. He's been working in his mindset for so long, I been working the way I been working for so long, the chemistry didn't really mix the way we thought it would."

Offering more of an insider's explanation into why the collaboration didn't bear out, Dre's co-producer Mel Man explained that "Rakim left due to a number of reasons. The main reason is that it just wasn't meant to be. Everyone involved is partially to blame (me included). There was so much hype about this album that a lot of pressure was put on before and during the recording of the album…Rakim never wanted to do a pop album, a pop single, or a gangster rap album. Those three things definably put a strain on getting Interscope's full backing and promotion for the album. For the record Dre never personally requested Rakim to 'get the guns out.' Dre wants every artist to be themselves and won't ever ask them to change who they are. However Dre knew that 'Oh My God' would never come out until Interscope got the album they wanted so it really put him in a tough spot. Dre and Rakim really struggled finding a way to balance things out and make the album Dre and Rakim wanted while at the same time make the album Interscope wanted…Rakim also didn't really want hooks. Songs without hooks somehow aren't good enough these days. Never mind that Rakim's greatest songs never really had hooks. Making pop hooks was not something Rakim was good at, so he struggled in that area. Rakim is by far the most talented rapper I have ever heard. Rakim is a lyricist not a hook writer. And there was no way Rakim would ever let someone write a hook for him.

So that was another problem. So there definitely were conflicts there. Dre and Ra could never come up with the balance they needed and it was really tough on both of them. In the end, Dre and Ra realized that it was going to be really tough to do the music they wanted and get Interscope's approval and their machine behind the release. So I disagree with Rakim saying he and Dre had creative differences. Ra and Dre simply could never find a way to make Interscope happy and yet make an album they themselves were happy with. I think Rakim would really get frustrated by Interscope's wishes and really struggled with preparing himself the way he needed to put 100% of himself into making the record.

The thing with Dre is that he expects his artists to be there when asked and be ready to work as hard as they ever had before. Rakim is a very cool cat, but at the same time kind of an enigma. Some days he would be gung ho ready to go and other days he would be hesitant or not in the studio. When he was focused Rakim was pure magic. When he wasn't he was hard to figure out. Common thought is that only a few tracks were recorded for 'Oh My God'. That is false. We may not have got a lot of full songs with vocals recorded (although we did more than has been reported), but we created a lot of instrumentals with Rakim in mind. Like Dre, Rakim is very picky in the beats and sometimes he would pass on beats that we thought were perfect. However the shit Ra and Dre did do together were mind blowing. I wish you could of heard it. I would get crazy excited when those two were orchestrating tracks together. I was convinced that a classic was being created. In the end though it just didn't work out...Like I said it just wasn't meant to be. Let's just keep our fingers crossed that a new version of 'Oh My God' gets released someday with a few tracks featuring the greatest mc ever and the greatest rap producer ever working their magic together."

Dr. Dre in the Studio

"Dre don't care about pushing a certain coast. He is all about finding talent and making good music no matter if you live in China or Compton."

—Mel Man, Dr. Dre Co-Producer on 'The Chronic 2001'

Chapter 12
50 Cent

Since Dre had signed Eminem in 1998 to his Aftermath Entertainment label, the two had created a hip-hop monopoly, but it wasn't until they collectively signed 50 Cent that Aftermath became a cottage industry. Dre had done it once before with Death Row Records in the early 1990s, but the 50 Cent signing was the millennium's equivalent of Suge Knight signing Tupac Shakur, only this time it was Dre who was cleaning up. It was his time now, but the stars had also lined up for Eminem, who had brought 50 Cent to Dre's attention and co-signed him to Shady Records, as well as for 50 himself, who was experiencing a rebirth of sorts after almost watching his career chances flatline with him literally after a now-legendary near-fatal shooting in 2000. While 50 was recouping and rebuilding his strength and arsenal (both lyrically and as a hustler), Dre and Em were laying their own groundwork for the greatness that would follow for all—constructing the foundation for what would become hip hop's first Roman Empire.

Talent had always gravitated toward Dre, but with Em as hip hop's new rainmaker, he had an ear to the street that was exclusive to his own generation of rising emcees, all admiring and aspiring to achieve even a slice of what Eminem had in his meteoric takeover of hip hop in the late 1990s and early years of the millennium. Dre could afford to hang back a little and let Eminem take point on the public side of promoting 50 Cent's transition from New York to the nation's hottest rap sensation.

Considering the top-shelf brand that Aftermath Entertainment had to offer, in terms both of exposure, muscle, hustle, and credibility, 50 knew he would need all of the above to pave a future for him that would guarantee the kind of greatness his talent commanded. The public presentation of 50's 'discovery' by rap's hottest commodity, Em, was key to establishing him as a legitimate 'protégé, wherein rap fans would embrace 50 no-questions-asked, giving him the instant credibility and therein sales that they had Eminem back in 1999 when Dre 'put Em on.'

The same strategy was at work with 50's signing, wherein a heavy, corporate machinery at work behind the curtains, the signing of 50 was a team effort, and Em and Dre were happy to play along where they had to, as they all stood to make a fortune. Eminem's label, Shady Records, was distributed through Aftermath, and thereafter through Interscope, such that Eminem owned a quarter stake in 50's contract, Dre a quarter, and Interscope the other half.

No matter the numbers, to the hip hop public, it was ultimately Eminem's visible fascination with 50's unique delivery and style, coupled with the anticipation of Dre's production, that got the buzz circulating on the street about 50 as fast as it did. As 50 explained the entire deal's unfolding, "Theo, my attorney, and Paul Rosenberg, Eminem's attorney and management, work

Chapter 12. 50 Cent

closely together—they grew up and kind of came up together. And I gave them a CD I put out called 'Guess Who's Back' and Em was in the middle of finishing The Eminem Show, and when he was done he got a chance to listen to it and at the time he was saying that he was kind of bored with what was going on with the same crews, the same artists, and that he wanted to do something different. When he had the opportunity to listen to it, he was like, 'Yo, this is it right here.' So, when he heard it, he was excited. So he took it to Dre, and they had me fly out. He called me on a Friday at 9 o'clock at night and was like, 'Yo, we need you to come out and meet with us tomorrow. What was weird was, like, I got the call on Friday at 9 o'clock at night and they wanted me to fly out the next day. I had other offers on the table from other companies like Universal, J Records, Jive Records, Warner Bros., Capitol, a few other companies—you know, those situations take place from 9 to 5 and Monday through Friday, like during your working hours. It felt a little different, so I flew out met with them the following day in an editing studio, and Dre stopped by and we kicked it, and when I left, I knew I was doing the deal with them, which ended up being for a $1 million advance. So I got back to the city, and then the offers skyrocketed: The offers were all the way up to a 1.6 million once the companies realized that Dr. Dre and Eminem were interested. I wasn't that excited with the initial phone call because I had (been to) so many meetings before that it really wasn't (fun). The creative part is my pleasure, the fun part for me. With business, you have to be able to separate the (artistry). Some artists are so into the (art form), they might as well be painters with a smock and French accent because they're going to get ripped off. Some people's talent is to write music or sing, or rap and other people's talent is to take advantage of those people. The numbers just went crazy. But when I had left (the meeting with Em and Dre), I had made this decision that I wanted to be on Shady/Aftermath, before I left just cuz the idea of being signed to them, of not having anyone trying to censor me, was a great idea. For everything else that comes with being successful as an artist. The notoriety—for people to recognize your talent. At the end of the day I felt like just sayin' Eminem's sales weren't strugglin' Dr Dre's sales weren't strugglin' and I felt like it was because they were putting together the type of projects that have been really quality projects! It was cool, I did the deal for like, a million dollars, but I still gained so much more out of working with Eminem and Dr. Dre that the other change for me means nothing. I'm in a good space right now."

While 50 may have been in a good place, the industry itself was not, rather in desperate need of a sales boost. 2002 had been the weakest year in sales for hip hop of the past five, and much of the sales strength of those had been driven by Dre's comeback. The only major label recording artist who did big numbers that year was Eminem, 50's label boss, and once word of the signing got out, everyone's hopes shot through the roof, along with the odds that 50 would meet and exceed those expectations. No one was more excited than Eminem himself about 50's prospects for greatness, "I kept hearing things (about 50), then my manager hit me off with a CD. I had been in a slump, thinking 'Where's hip hop gonna go? When I heard 50's stuff, it was like 'Ok, let's see who 50's talking to now? Let's see what the story is on him?'...(Now with his album), I'm there doing the mix downs and me and Dre are just overseeing the whole project, making sure that every song is hot...I wish my first album was this hot. That's all I can say. I'm not selling the album. The album is going to sell itself."

Dre echoed Em's sentiments on 50's promise as the next great step in hip hop's evolution artistically and commercially, "50 came out here to L.A. for a couple of days and he seemed like he was cool as shit. 50 is one of the most incredible artists I worked with as far as writing, basic performance and vibing. He came in, and every track I put up, he had something for it. He wrote to it. He got in the booth and did his thing. 50's album in my opinion is gonna compete with all the classic hip-hop Lps that came out in the last 10 years. It's right up there. Shit came out hot."

As rappers, the respect between Eminem and 50 seemed authentically mutual, as 50 explained, "I'm *almost* the hottest rapper…I signed a deal with the hottest rapper. Eminem is so talented, it's annoying—he got a gift. If you believe in God, you believe in fate, and I think he's exactly what God intended him to be. You can look at him and see what he's doing on television and he's doing whatever shit he's doing and however the script should be or however the video director chose the set is what you see, but when you kick it with him and you kind of get to know him and you work alongside him, he's not even into this shit. He's into music, he just wants to make music. And the success that comes with it, your head might be so big—I know I'd be running around, you'd all probably have to tap me on the shoulder to turn my head because it's so big, my hat won't fit. But he's the biggest artist there right now, and from my experience, from what I see from being around him, he gets more enjoyment out of making the music than he does out of seeing what it actually does in numbers after he's done with it. I think Eminem is the best…period. The best. I'm starting to figure it out. I think that what happened to Em happened so fast that he hasn't even really realized how big he is. He's still down-to-earth and humble, despite the fact that he can rap circles around the game. He's so talented sometimes it can become annoying. Plus he can't really toot his own horn, it makes people uneasy; but I can. The boy is No. 1. We're alike in a lot of ways, he speaks a lot from his life experience, otherwise you wouldn't know who Kim was. I do the same, it's just a little more gunplay, more life-threatening situations...He may not be my favorite person to listen to all the time, but he does rap about his real life issues. If not you wouldn't know how he feels about his mother, who Hailey is, who Kim is. Those situations—he's using his real life situations (in his raps), and that's what I do. You see what I'm sayin'? So I respect it when I listen to it. I enjoy it cuz it's really what's going on with him and how he feels, he's expressing it through his music. I do the same thing. So I look at and go 'He's one of the best to me like when I listen to him.' And then I get to work beside him so I know how much he puts into how his music comes out. He's a perfectionist, he (and) Dre (are) really perfectionists."

Once all the contracts were signed and advances disbursed, 50 went into the studio to begin work on what would become the biggest selling hip hop album of 2003. For 50, the creative process moved along as seamlessly as his signing with Em and Dre had, wherein the environment was one in which "it exceeded my expectations. It's more than I ever thought it would be. It's almost to the point where we're not working. It's that easy. Everyone knows exactly what they're supposed to do and they're executing (it). Shit just got done so fast. I had 48 records recorded prior to the deal being done. They took 16 records of the 48 that they felt like had to stay...I got a lot of extra music so I can use them on soundtracks and other placements...I got the best rappers, best producers around me...Its' the best music that I've recorded to date, I've got the best production—Dr. Dre, Eminem, Roc Wilder Twee Lo, Diggah...I'm getting better! This is like my album will be twice as good as my last album. Where I'm at right now I don't even see anybody. My competition is just to fit in with Eminem and Dre...My album is so well put together. Eminem says he wishes his first album was like mine. (Instead of) comparing it to classics like, *Illmatic* or

Reasonable Doubt, he said that this album sounds like an album that's made after you know exactly what you're doing…I'm not even trying to keep up with anyone else in the music business outside of Em and Dre."

On another level entirely, 50 definitely felt confident in the aftermath of signing with Dre and Em that he had made the right career decision, "One thing I know for sure is that I'm content with myself. I see the expectations that people have around me already since I signed the deal (with Shady Records). It makes no difference to me when people sit around and wishing for me to do bad, I'm already doing better than people around me would expect. I'm already on cloud 9, I'm floating." Things moved fast for 50 once he signed the deal, such that "I started right after we signed. They tripped on me because I sent 12 at a time. I didn't want them to listen to so much at once that they couldn't pick what they liked, so I sent 12 at a time. After they listened to (those) records, they decided we're going to do a few more records and that's it. I went to Los Angeles. I was there for five days. I recorded seven records with Dre and then I went to Detroit and did six more records with Em. Four records went on the 8 Mile Soundtrack but we've done some more records since then." Ultimately, 50's goal in the course of recording his debut album under the deal seemed to be to stay on a competitive level with his mentors, providing him with a constant motivation to give only his best, "I fear not fitting in with Eminem and Dr. Dre. That's what counts to me. The other stuff (the threat of violence) has already been a part of my life, none of that is new. They signed me, so I'll never be equivalent to Eminem or Dr. Dre. If Em says 'I'm the future of music', then what he's saying is he's the future of music because he signed me."

Finally, 50 also seemed to take the notion that he could become hip hop's next overnight icon as seriously from a business point of view as his backers were, wherein he was conscious of the fact that he had been handed a one in a million shot that he couldn't afford to blow, "(Interscope CEO) Jimmy Iovine will tell me, 'I hope you're smart like Dre.' Dre will pull me to the side and tell me to stay focused. I told him in the beginning that my intentions weren't to be trouble. Nobody wants to buy a problem. And with my background, there's a possibility that they'd be purchasing the biggest problem that they've ever found. But because they believed me when I told them I wanted to make music, we were able to progress."

With all the elements brewing properly, the chemistry between 50 as the artist and 50 the commodity were blending according to formula, and with the proper support network in place, the most potent and sometimes unpredictable part of that recipe for greatness, the creation of hit records, was also going off without a hitch. For 50, in terms of working with the Godfather of hip hop production, the rapper was in creative heaven as an artist, coupled with the fact that there was nothing contrived about the experience from an A&R perspective, leaving 50 free to be himself in the studio and in the context of art-imitating-life. The latter, as much as 50 was watching himself outside of the studio to make sure he stayed clear of trouble, was still an important element to his undeniable authenticity as a rapper, such that it needed to be credibly translated in the lab, "production-wise, I don't think there's a producer better than Dr. Dre, especially for me. He's from NWA—that's like the original gangsta rap group. How he not going to understand my lyrical content? When it gets a little edgy, he gets excited. He's not going, 'Yo, I don't know if you should say that.' He's not calling me in going, 'I think we should switch this line.' I ain't have no boundaries. Em never says 'Don't say that' or 'Can you change that?' If anything, they are always saying that to him. And Dre, he's got to understand what I'm doing, he's from NWA. When I was on

Columbia and I dropped 'How To Rob,' they actually told me not to cut my hair. They thought I was supposed to look like Ol' Dirty Bastard. Just dirty, like, 'You crazy, like the guy who said they would rob everybody.' I couldn't even get it. Like Ol' Dirty Bastard did this record, like how are they supposed to know who I am when I shoot 'Thug Love,' which is the real single for this record? What is it going to look like? What are we going to do? We going to do Trading Places? 'Hey, Mortimer!' Like somebody going to throw some money on the floor and I'm going to change into the new kid? It was just a record, and they wanted to make that the theme with me as an artist, period. I'm not with that. Columbia, I don't think that they understood me, period."

Continuing, 50 explained that "Dr. Dre and Eminem, they made the final executive decision. I told them what I wanted and we kinda shifted through them. I recorded 12 w/ Dre and I only put 4 on the album so I got plenty of records…With Dre its like, I do vocals, I write the vocals and then Dre would come and we'd do vocals, like we change, not too much, but if he feels like I could say something a lil differently, we'll change that. Dre, he'll play dope beats—they're automatic, (He'll say), 'These are the hits, 50. So pick one of these and make a couple of singles or something.' The very first time he heard (me rap on) 'In Da Club' he said, 'Yo, I didn't think you was going to go *there* with it, but, you know, it works.' He was probably thinking of going in a different direction with that song. Then he expanded it into a hit record. (Dre and Em) made me a lot better, fast… Creatively, it's a better space for me." For 50, the trust he felt artistically with both Dre and Eminem seemed equally as important as the freedom they gave him there, which 50 qualified by explaining that he felt that trust as implicitly as he did because all three artists were on the same level, "I think Shady/Aftermath is way better than Columbia…re understands being from NWA, my lyrical content. And Eminem, picture him saying 'Yo you can't say that.' He's as edgy as you get on his level, so he understands exactly what it is and I think that's what drew him to me—you know when he heard the music. He know what it is, so it's cool. I'm real comfortable (because of that), the work process is—I'll go do it and they'll listen and then they'll say 'Yo, you know what I think you should do, something like this,' and I'll take their advice and pass the world of respect. Cause I know that for sure they are really in my best interest. They are my corner for real. If they didn't come get me to do the deal, what would I be doin?" The unsettling subtext of the latter question lies in the sobering look it provides into the hustler psychology that truly authentic street rappers live by, wherein, as 50 explained, "I ain't got no Plan B. I ain't never had no job before. My plan wasn't working. I've never even had working papers before. So it was either this or hustling. So I had to do my thing."

Eminem, in addition to being 50's label boss, was so excited about the opportunity to work with a rapper of 50's talent, that the great white hope threw his own hat into the ring as a producer on several of the tracks. 50 had no problem with this because he seemed to be genuinely impressed with Eminem's skills as a producer, such that "Em is so talented it becomes annoying...Every time we go to the studio, he's got something new to play and it's like, 'Oh man, I gotta have something new to play, too.' Em is the rapper's rapper. He listens to everything. Every word, every slang, if you change something he's going to hear it all, (and that comes out in his producing.)"

In describing the process of working with Em as a producer, 50 explained, "Em, he spins records and like he sends me a skeleton and I'll write to it. Then we'll build the song around it...He usually likes to watch me do what I'm doing. He lets me just do what I want. You know what he'll do? He'll send a skeleton—like the track won't be finished when I get it. I'll rap to a beat that's not even 50 percent done and I'll put the concept down. And then he'll build the record around what I did...At the end of the day, it's not until he actually mixes the record that you'll hear what it is for real. And I've been happy with everything that we've done so far. He mixed a lot of records on this album. He produced and mixed his two records and then he mixed, I think, about five or six other records on the album. He can expand the record. He can make it something that, if someone else has already produced the base of it, he can put what it takes to make it go over the top."

As Eminem explained from a production angle, working with 50 is a dream because "there's not much fixing involved, which is a beautiful thing." In the course of 50's experience collaborating creatively with Dr. Dre and Eminem, the rapper was clearly a student, explaining that, through serious study, trial and error, the duo's magic is "starting to rub off cuz I start to make sure before I send them a record, (its up to their standards.) Cause (before) I would do a record and send it to them to see what they think, and now I kinda put it together better because—(for example), after Dre records vocals with you, you pick up things from him, cause he's the best producer I've ever worked with. And when you record with someone and they change your process, it means you learn something in that situation, so now when I go in the booth and record records on my own, (I got it down.) They could be in LA, Em could be in Detroit and I'm working on a record here, I kind of record it how I think Dre would do it, you see what I'm sayin'? So I know that I'm pickin up new things from being around them, and they should expect my music to be even better…I worked with, you know, some good producers—like, I was with the Trackmasters for a little bit, and. I had all of them. But Dre is a different type…I haven't worked with a producer that was more comfortable with me doing whatever I want to do."

Elaborating on Dre and 50's creative process, collaborator Mike Elizondo described the process by which 'In Da Club' was invented, explaining that "(Dre & I) actually wrote the track six months before, but the artist we were working on at the time passed on it…But we felt strongly about the track, so we stashed it away until we played it for 50 (Cent). He loved it, and he fiercely started writing the lyrics. About an hour later, 50 had written the entire lyric. He came back in the room and started singing (the now famous intro) 'Go Shorty, it's your birthday, we're gonna party like, it's your birthday'."

Once word of 50's signing got out on the street, fans were instantly hungry for anything they could get their hands on in the way of material from the rapper, and while New York fans had the benefit of the mix tape market, where 50 had made his underground come up, the suburban hip hop fans, which constitute roughly 60% of the consumer market for the genre, would soon get their fix.

Chapter 12. 50 Cent

In perfect timing, Eminem's signing of 50 Cent coincided with the upcoming release of the rapper's debut film, '8 Mile', the soundtrack of which was being released on Shade Records. A sure-fire hit with fans, Dre, Em and Interscope made sure the soundtrack was 50 Cent heavy on material, knowing they could not have asked for a more ideal vehicle by which to introduce 50 Cent to the public in lieu of the release of his debut LP.

50's breakout hit from the soundtrack was 'Wanksta', which the rapper himself explained as "my joint, right there. That's the first one that broke for me off the 8 Mile joint. I'm happy with that, like for me and sales on the soundtrack. It took off by itself, we was gonna do 'Places To Go' at first and then the record. We started on the mixtape with it and then Funkmaster Flex got it and he liked the record and they just went crazy on it. You know? So it worked out for me I'm blessed with that." Elaborating on the process for choosing which songs would be included on '8 Mile' to introduce 50, the rapper reveals that he played an integral role in choosing the tracks, but also points out that the whole process was inspired, such that greatness was hanging overhead the whole time, " 'Me I Call The Shots Round Here', that was off the '8 Mile' Soundtrack too. Actually, Rakim wrote to that record and I did it over, you know…That's a Dre joint and I took the beat, cause that's what I do—I take the beats. I did it over cause I thought the beat was hot and I put my own song together on it. (But it's crazy that it was Rakim's first)."

The core of '8 Mile' focuses on the street art of battle rapping, known in the hip hop underground as 'battling', the premier way to make a name for oneself as an emcee on the street level, and the vehicle by which Eminem first came up in Detroit's hip hop underground. While this type of contest is also popular in New York and around the country, as it has been for years prior to the release of '8 Mile', 50 Cent, ironically, never made his name this way, preferring the mix-tape route for one bottom line reason, there was money involved. As he explains, in true hustler fashion, "No, I never battled. You know why? Because I never (saw) any money in battling. To be honest with you, I'm from the bottom. The music business is a business where no (prerequisites) are necessary. Eminem is a drop out, I'm a drop out, and we both making more money than our high school teachers do."

With 50 and Eminem linked at the hip in the media, rap pundits and critics naturally sought to compare the two, a tendency that 50 saw as natural when the player-hater factor was considered, such that "more people hate Eminem than 50 Cent because Eminem is number one…It's just a different class of people that hate Eminem (than hate me). People that hate Eminem get a headache every time they see his face because he's so good. You got actors out there that still don't have films that break $100 million, but Eminem (did that on his) first go around."

For 50 Cent, the bottom line in terms of the media comparisons between him and Em was that it gave 50 that much more to live up to creatively and commercially on an overall level with critics, fans, and executives, while personally, setting a certain bar for himself to achieve what his mentors had on all relevant levels. 50 clearly had the confidence as an artist, due in large part to the support system he had at work for him behind the scenes. Within his personal life, 50's most immediate personal life change seemed to be his most desired when he had first signed with Em and Dre, that being "I ain't gotta worry about bills...Finances changed a lot."

The fringe benefit of groupie love also suited the rapper just fine, such that "I feel like I got a facelift...The ho's they treat me so much better...I'm eligible (now) for a whole lot of women that I'm not eligible for. They found that them checks get cut, things get different. Like I look better or something, they treat me better." Aware of the role his overnight celebrity had played in securing the additional trim, 50 seemed to be receiving the attention from the right perspective, such that "you just take it in stride.

Yeah, it's fun...I mean as long as you know why the situation is happening, you be alright." Perhaps hip hop's most resilient new emcee, 50 Cent's signing with Shady/Aftermath would go onto revitalize hip hop's sales slump with the 2003 release of 'Get Rich or Die Trying', and most importantly, inject the reality back into rap. 50 was already on top of the world, on his way into the outer space of stardom. What many hip hop fans didn't know was that he'd spent years getting there, and had gotten his start from another hip hop legend.

'Get Rich or Die Trying' was released nationally on Friday, February 6, 2003, four days before the traditional Tuesday album release, in an unusual industry move designed to combat the very bootleg/mixtape market that had given 50 the street buzz he was riding high on. With a major label debut that entered (not surprisingly) at # 1 on the *Billboard* Top 200 Album Chart, 50 Cent sold 872,000 copies nationally in his first week as a major label artist, and would go onto sell 1.7 million copies of 'Get Rich' by the end of its second week in release. Ultimately, the record would sell upward of 4.3 million copies in just 12 weeks, rivaling only mentors Eminem and the late Tupac Shakur in soundscan's record books for a hip hop release.

Reflecting on the album's sensational success only a few months after its release, in the late spring of 2003, 50 admitted that, despite his confidence on tape and in the media regarding his rise to hip hop's premier spot, "I didn't anticipate selling that many records...I sold 872,000 copies my first week. It's almost normal for artists to drop like 35 percent in sales the following week. I came back and did 822,000 the next week, so I was shocked." The rest of the record buying world, however, was not, and couldn't get enough of 50-Mania.

While Dr. Dre-produced first single 'In Da Club' shot to the top of the Billboard Pop Singles Chart, and remained there for weeks, 50 quickly followed up with '21 Questions', which quickly joined its predecessor in the top 10, giving 50 Cent 2 top ten singles simultaneously, a new record for a debut hip hop artist. Dr. Dre's empire was growing exponentially—in both cultural influence and sales revenues—and it seemed with 50 Cent, Dre had truly come full-circle in establishing the third—or perhaps even the fourth—generation of hip hop founded on his signature sound.

> "*I have to feel it (to know when a record's going to be a hit.)...I get this little tingling sensation in my balls and shit. Then I know it's right.*"
>
> —Dr. Dre

Chapter 13
2002 —2005

By 2002, Dre had his new producing routine down to a science, such that he even become a student again, seeming to be searching for new ways to keep things in advance of what he had made the current popular sound of hip hop. His studies included taking piano lessons, studying music theory, and even plotting the signing of a ghetto rock band to Aftermath, and even studying music theory, explaining regarding the latter that "(studying music theory has) actually broadened the way I look at music and listen to it, just knowing how the notes are placed. I pay attention to all that a little bit more now. A while back, I thought it would hurt me, I thought I would start paying too close attention, and maybe miss something. But I think it's helping out. And once I really get that shit, 'Look out!'"

In the studio however, things remained largely the same foundationally in terms of his method for creating a constantly fluid musical environment where the magic happened. Among those recording routines, which allowed Dre to have, no boundaries were a series of five MC3000's he kept lined up and running at all times, explaining that "I love using the MPC3000. I like setting up like four or five different MPC3000's, so I don't have to keep changing disks. So I have them all lined up, and I have different drum sounds in each one, and then we use one for sequencing the keyboard."

With almost a creative family of collaborators surrounding him in collaborators like Mike Elizondo, Colin Wolfe, Mike Simms, Sean Thomas, T green, Scott Storch, Camara Kamron, Larry 'Uncle' Chapman, and Maurico 'Veto' Iragorri among others, Dre explained that "I am a perfectionist, but it has a lot to do with the people that are around you. They have to have the same vision, the same motivation…(My) engineer is very important. Working with me, the engineer's almost got to have ESP to know what I'm thinking, and he has that. It's like body language, he can almost feel what I'm getting ready to ask him for. It's a building process, and it took us a while to get to that point. We've been working together for years, probably since '98 or '99…It takes a while to get the right people around you; it takes a long time. But I think I've finally done it, I think this is going to be my crew for a while."

While Dre felt he had settled on his creative team, as for their sound, his approach to settling on a final mix of any single was much more open ended, occurring only when he reached "a feeling I get when it's right, so I just keep going until I get that feeling. It's like a butterfly type feeling. When I hit it, and it's right, and the mix is right, that's when it's time to come out. Nothing leaves this studio until I get that feeling…I don't go out to clubs and party like I used to. I just get up, go to the gym, come to the studio. Usually I get to the studio around 3 PM, and my hours can vary anywhere from two hours to, I mean, my record is 79 hours non stop. As long as the ideas are flowing, I'm in here…I want somebody that's gonna come in and work, and be ready to fucking really do they thing. Because I'm the first one here, and I'm the last one to leave, I tell 'em, 'You can't work harder than me, but try to keep up.' I feel when I come to the studio, I have the same energy today as I did 20 years ago when I started. I still feel it, I love music...Just music in general, man. I love making music. This is what I was put here to do, to make music. I love doing this, man, it's almost like a high for me. If I'm out of the studio too long, it feels funny. I got this feeling like, 'Damn, this could have been the day I came up with fucking 'Billie Jean' or some shit.' If I'm not in the studio, it always crosses my mind."

While Dre was willing to spend hours laboring away in the studio chasing the perfect sound, his process for creating hit records had an entirely different and more instinctive birth process, with Dre explaining that "right off (I know if something's a hit.) Like I said, it's a feeling. Most of the time that record comes fast. It's not one of those things where you're working on the same record for two weeks, usually that record comes in a couple of hours."

Elaborating on the work ethic he expected from himself and his team of collaborators, Dre explained that his philosophy was to lead by example, such that "you got to come in and go to work, man. I open the door, like I said, you're not going to work harder than me. The harder you work, the harder I'm going to work. At least I'm going to try to make sure that's happening...I think some people that I've worked with expect to come in and for me to wave a magic wand and say, 'Ding, hit record!' But it's not like that. You have to come in and give some energy, and we have to put the same amount of work in on the record. It's not just going to be me putting my hand in your back and moving you around like a puppet."

One recording norm Dre had finally come to terms with utilizing in the course of recording was Protools, explaining that "I had Pro Tools right when it came out, but I wasn't a fan of it because I lost a little bit of my low end before they perfected it. So, I used to just use Pro Tools for sequencing the albums. But now I think they've perfected it enough for me to roll with it, so I've been using it quite a bit."

Discussing the method by which he constructed the foundation (i.e. the drums, an element of any Dr. Dre hit that had always been revered in and of itself) of any of his dozens of multi-platinum sonic masterpieces, Dre explained that "we really take a lot of time on getting the right drum sounds. We EQ the drums before we sample them into the MPC, and then once we come up with the track, we spend a lot of time EQing the drums before we record them into Pro Tools. We take quite a bit of time to get that right, because I know it's one of the things that people like about my music. I've used the same drum sounds on a couple of different songs on one album before but you'd never be able to tell the difference because of the EQ."

Elaborating on his building process, Dre addressed the distinctive presence of keyboards in his sound by revealing that as futuristic as many of his tracks sounded, "I love the old school sounds. ARP String Ensemble, Rhodes, old school Clavinet, the whole shit. I'm a big keyboard fan. I don't really dig working with samples because you're so limited when you sample."

Broadening the explanation of the technical side of the process involved in building Dre's wall of sound, engineer Maurico 'Veto' Iragorri explained that "the brain of (any Dr. Dre recording session) is the MIDI sequencer, the Akai MPC3000. We use the Korg Triton keyboard. Usually that's the controller—the Nord Lead and Korg's MS2000. Lately we've been trying out the Alesis Andromeda A6. Someone recommended a Waldorf cue, and we seem to like that one as well. They let us try it for a day and we said, 'Yes, we'll keep it!' You might also find a nice array of vintage keyboards on hand, including those by Rhodes, Wurlitzer, Moog, and Roland."

Not surprisingly, Dre's work ethic was motivated in large part by the fact that he got bored quickly with what was on the radio, so much so at the time that "I don't think I'm really inspired by anything that's going on out there right now. I'm not really mad at it, but there's nothing that's really motivating me right now except for the artists I'm working with. I'm not just saying that because they're with my label. These artists are coming in with some hot new ideas so it's just the stuff that I'm working with that's inspiring. There's nothing out there that's really different. There's nobody doing or saying anything that I haven't heard before… That's exactly what I do; I try to reinvent myself. If you keep doing the same thing, people are going to get tired of it, that's when it becomes old. So, I gotta keep reinventing myself."

Some of the new ground that Dre hoped to cover during this period involved film scoring, explaining that "I started studying music theory, learning how to read and write music. It's been over two years, so I'm really getting involved in that. I definitely want to get into scoring movies. I have to have the knowledge, so I think in the next four or five years I'll have it down, I'll be ready. I'm not even going to attempt to do something if I don't think I'm going to be great at it. I know for a fact that's something that I could be good at, but I have to get the knowledge first. That's almost like learning a new language. I have to really understand what I'm doing, I have to learn that language. It takes a while, and I want to be the best at it, so I'm going to put the time in…(I also hooked up with Burt Bacharach), we did a little thing together. My piano teacher introduced us. Burt Bacharach came by the studio, and we chopped it up for a little while. I gave him a couple of skeleton tracks on a CD, and he went home and played some piano over it. The next thing I know they had this jazz trumpet player play on the record, and it sounded hot. I think they're going to put it out. I would like to really get in, and do something from scratch with him as opposed to me giving him a track, and him going to his studio and doing his thing, and us sending it back and forth."

Dre's willingness to experiment to the extreme of collaborating with a classical music composer reflected how advanced his mind was ahead of the game's own, which couldn't seem to think for itself without Dre's input. As the Dr. viewed the latter, "when I put a record out, I think a lot of people are influenced by my music, and I think there's a lot of shit that comes out that sounds similar to mine. That makes the sound become old a little bit faster, so I definitely have to keep reinventing myself and trying new things."

Among other new things Dre tried was introducing some new faces into the Aftermath production fold, including up and coming engineers/producers like Focus, Hi-Tek, Jonathan 'J.R.' Rotem, and Ron Feemstar. Focus offered through discussion of the specific process which defined his creative collaboration with Dre, some additionally unique insight into the producer's recording process, explaining that "(when I was first working with him on Aftermath productions in general, Dre) was in one room and I was in another. He would come and check on me from time to time making sure I was serious about this music…He's no joke. That man is the epitome of a perfectionist. I love that about his work ethic. That's why he gets the results he gets. Fans know he won't put out no bullshit. Dre takes his time.… Dre knows what it takes to make a hit. Not a one hit wonder He is a living legend. You can't start putting out bullshit because people will hate you and move to the next cat. Dre has a lot of things in store for the industry…(When) we've worked…together, he is VERY particular. We actually started a beat from scratch and he eq'd everything to damn near sound like a record. No roughs! He paints the picture and wants to see and hear exactly what's in his head. I dig that yo. I'm just like that and watching him. Let's me know I'm not wrong being this way…Dre would never hold me back. He wants us to grow."

Hi-Tek, for his part, described working alongside Dr. Dre as an experience in which "I've been working with Dr. Dre on a lot of Aftermath projects. I've been on the Lloyd Banks, 50 Cent, and that's all been through the relationship with Dr. Dre and G-Unit…(Originally), I sent a CD to Dub-C for his album (Westside Connection), and Dre got a hold of it…Dre heard the CD that I gave him and there was a track on there that he wanted for 'Truth Hurts'. Ever since then…I've just been working with him. I've gotten involved in a lot of projects…He's not really working with every producer in the game. He really gave me a nice block. That's pretty much all I know….I think from the time I shook his hand he really upped my game. Just meeting him and seeing the equipment that he works on just gave me that insight. Like, 'Damn, I'm basically there.' It just upped my game mentally. Just watching him and listening to him, seeing how tracks start and seeing how he completes them. Once I hear the finished product I get a good idea of how to beef the track up and give it that real clarity and make it a great song. I definitely learned a lot from the time I met him."

As freshmen members of the Aftermath team, Focus described some of the individual production ingredients that each bring to the table to sweeten the mix, explaining that "Tek and I incorporate that East coast flav into the west coast driven rhythms that make up the math. Tek is from Cincinnati and he's an incredible producer, too. I love his stuff. Mel helped create the Math's signature sound so all of us together is a force to be reckoned with."

Ron Feemstar, another newer member of the Aftermath production roster, first began working with Dre during production for 'The Eminem Show' on cuts including 'Business,' 'When The Music Stops,' 'Say What You Say' and 'My Dad's Gone Crazy.' Describing their creative process in the studio as one in which "We started writing and recording in Reno, then we went to Detroit. Then we finished working in LA. It was a lot of fun. Dre would do the beats, Eminem would write the raps, and I would work on the music with Mike Elizondo (on three of the songs). I helped dress up the music with piano, strings, harpsichord and other instruments…It was great working with Eminem, his vibe and talent is amazing…(Next), We started working with 50 Cent and Mary J. Blige about the same time…Dre hooked me up with 50 Cent, and we worked with 50 through the end of the year and into 2003. I (co-wrote) two songs with 50, including the single 'If I Can't.' Dre, Mike and I also worked with Mary, on the song 'Not Today' (which is a duet with Eve)." Finally, Jonathan 'J.R.' Rotem, one of Dre's busier collaborators within the Aftermath camp, explained that he feels he belongs a part of the Aftermath family because "Dr. Dre's production is what really inspired me to want to produce hip hop…Being one of the producer/keyboardists in LA, we hooked up through mutual contacts, as the game is not that big. Initially, after an 'audition', we discussed me playing keys for him when he was starting Detox about a year ago… There's people who have a lot of skills that I could learn from, so I'm at the very beginning. I'm trying to learn all I can,

Chapter 13. 2002—2005

about workin with artists and really learn what makes a song. There's people who play keyboards, there's people who make beats, and there's producers, and a producer is somebody who puts it all together. So yes, it helps that I can play keys and make all the beats, so I can play everything. But in the end that's not what really makes a good producer. A good producer is somebody who starts from nothing and turns stuff into a hit. Somebody who sees the whole process from start to finish. So I think in that definition of a producer, like...Dr. Dre...I have a long way to go and a lot to learn. But I'm very excited and very pleased with my accomplishments, but it's just infinite, there's a lot more to learn...(from) Dre, cause I was so influenced by him...On Detox I made a track that Dre heard. This was a while ago, cause he started 'Detox' a few times then he put it down to produce Game. This was right before he started going full time with Game. This was like a year ago. So he heard it and laid vocals to it. I heard a version where he laid vocals, and he sounded incredible on it...It was a very futuristic sounding track, and Dre was so excited about it that they bought it the next day. They wanted it that bad that they paid for it the next day. It was the first track that Dre laid vocals on for 'Detox'…Dre really sounded unbelievable on it, like a master and a veteran in the game…It's an incredible track with a lot of energy. I mean Dre's a perfectionist, so he's gonna record a lot of material before he selects what he's gonna put on his album…It was definitely one of my favorite tracks that I have ever done, and hearing Dr. Dre on it was just mind blowing…With Aftermath it's definitely a relationship that's building, but to be honest with you, I would say I wanted to build more, but ironically I've done a lot more work with G-Unit than I have with Aftermath. With G-Unit I've worked with Tony Yayo, I've worked with Olivia, I've worked with (Young) Buck, I've worked with 50. I've basically worked with everybody on G-Unit. OK, I've also worked with Game, who is on both. You know, I'm a huge fan of Aftermath, a huge fan of Dre, everybody on the label, Busta, Eve, everybody."

In terms of advice, Dre dispensed to any of his protégé producers, he reasoned that any producer should look at his work as "a job, man, that's all it is. I'm serious about music. It's a job, and I want to get paid of course, but I don't need to talk about it. If I was a plumber, I wouldn't talk about the money I was making, I'd just talk about my job. I'd be talking about pipes and shit. All I want to talk about is the music and how we can better it…I think we just need producers who are willing to stick their necks out there and try new and different things. I love Outkast and what they're doing because they're trying some new and different things, and it's working for them. They stick their necks out there, and it works and I love that. That's what we have to get more of."

One Aftermath producer who served as an example of Dre's formula successfully applied was Mike Elizondo, who between 2003 and 2004, was entering the busiest period of his production career, in many cases alongside Dre. His busy

Chapter 13. 2002—2005

production plate was a reflection of how seriously he'd taken to heart and applied Dre's philosophy toward producing records and work ethic in the course of developing his own craft. Elizondo and Dre's collaborate resume boasted the fact that they had co-written and produced 'In Da Club' by 50 Cent, and Eminem's 'Just Lose It' and 'The Real Slim Shady', 'Let Me Blow Ya Mind' by Eve (featuring Gwen Stefani), and 'Family Affair' by Mary J. Blige among others. In the broader scope of his collaboration with Dre, Elizondo had co-written three songs on the Marshall Mathers LP, four songs on the 'Eminem Show', and a staggering eight songs on the rapper's fourth album, 'Encore.' Additionally, he'd co-written six songs on 50 Cent's 'Get Rich Or Die Tryin' album by 50 Cent, as well as other platinum artists including Jay-Z, Busta Rhymes, Obie Trice, Game, Busta Rhymes, Snoop Dogg, D-12, Xzibit, Nate Dogg, Macy Gray, Nelly Furtado, Mandy Moore, Warren G and Truth Hurts.

Commenting on what was on his creative plans for 2004 and beyond—with Dre and independently as the Dr. would want him to in the course of establishing his own legacy—Elizondo explained that "with Dre, we're working on new material for Eminem, 50 Cent, Busta Rhymes, Eve, and a new artist called the Game. I'm producing Fiona Apple's next album, which we just started."

During this period in Dre's new renaissance, he also collaborated with a variety of artists, all of whom seemed to view their time working with Dre as a learning opportunity. One example of the latter was outlined by rapper Royce Da 5'9, who explained that "just being around him, Dre is one big ball of energy. You just learn everything that he's been through. The however many years he was in the game before I met him, it all shows in his energy. You pick up on it if you're the type to soak up game. I just learned my work ethic and how to stay in the studio at all times. I got my work ethic from being around Dre, because they're always in the studio."

Eminem protégé Obie Trice, who had the opportunity to work with Dre via his affiliation as an artist on Eminem's Shady Records, explained that "Going to L.A. with Dre was a learning experience, just seeing how the dude works and being up-close and personal with a dude whose music I appreciated growing up…To sit down with him and listen to the beats was just an unbelievable thing. I went in there and worked. He's a real dude…I definitely like his work ethic. I can see where Eminem get his from. Dre is the father of work ethic. You gotta get in there and you really gotta to work. When I go to work in the studio, I'm not there to bullshit around. I'm there to make music."

"Do hip-hop producers hold Dr. Dre in high esteem? It's like asking a Christian if he believes Christ died for his sins. Dre has a whole coast on his back...He discovered Snoop, signed Eminem, 50 Cent and now the Game. He takes artists with great potential and makes them even better. I wonder where I'd be right now if Dre had discovered me...I remember hearing Dre's music before I really knew who he was. I had a tape of Eazy-E's Eazy-Duz-It when I was ten years old...I didn't know what 'production' was back then, but I knew I loved the music. The more I learned about producing hip-hop, the more I respected what Dre was doing. Think about how on old N.W.A records the beat would change four or five times in a single song. A million people can program beats, but can they put together an entire album like it's a movie?...Dre's productions like Tupac's 'California Love' were just so far beyond what I was doing that I couldn't even comprehend what was going on. I had no idea how to get to that point, how to layer all those instruments. The Chronic is still the hip-hop equivalent to Stevie Wonder's Songs in the Key of Life. It's the benchmark you measure your album against if you're serious...(Dre's) the definition of a true talent: Dre feels like God placed him here to make music, and no matter what forces are aligned against him, he always ends up on the mountaintop."

—*Kanye West on Dr. Dre's influence and legacy in 2005*

Conclusion
Detox, 2006 and Beyond...

The term DETOX implies some form of withdrawal or retirement. The world of rap couldn't withdraw however from Dre's sound, they were permanently hooked. For his own part, Dr. Dre has made no secret in interviews of the fact that this would be his third and final solo album, the final piece of a trilogy that had defined the better part of twenty years of hip hop's commercial sound and creative direction. He'd gone back and forth publicly in interviews about whether he would ever release the album, in part perhaps because the thought of the permanence of retirement would scare any one at the top of their profession.

Dre sat on a throne, atop a kingdom that spanned the entire history of a musical genre, with a musical treasure chest with more jewels in the form of hits than any other presence had singularly had in the 25 years the producer had been in the game. He'd been responsible for more mini-musical revolutions than grooves on the records he spun, and had been the driving force behind a few legitimate, mainstream musical revolutions in that time as well. The whole time, Dre had remained in total control behind the console, steering his hip hop mothership into new musical frontier after another, exploring and pioneering new musical and sonic soundscapes that would never have been discovered, let alone developed without him.

In terms of opening the gateway to hip hop's next sonic universe, longtime Dre collaborator Mel Man explained the frustration in producing the album as simply a matter of a perfectionist seeking perfection, and settling for nothing less, such that "we are striving for 100% live instrumental tracks built completely from scratch which takes a lot of work since we do so many of them before Dre whittles them down later on…Dre pushes us to dig deep and put our own ideas into the skeleton instrumentals we have made alongside him for Detox over the last couple of years…The dilemma is how complex of tracks will the listening audience want to hear. Do they want orchestra like pieces or the tightly focused, yet simple beats you are used to from Dre. Ideally all of us and Dre want the most mindbending and complex original music experience ever heard on record…In the end I think you will hear elements of these complex beats but you won't hear the way they originally were created…Interscope is breathing down Dre's neck to get Detox out by year end. But Dre refuses to release it until he is ready."

Dre's own reasons for the album's delay in completion ranged from doubts the producer had about his own relevance as an emcee, with the producer arguing that "I'm 37 years old… I'm not talking about lowriders and blunts and all that anymore…I mean, that's played…What can I talk about?…As a matter of fact, I'm tired of hearing other people talk about it, to tell you the truth."

Another of his reasons involved Dre's claim that the level of success his label was operating at simply demanded too much of his creative and business schedule to allow him to devote the proper amount of time the project that his own standards dictated, explaining at one point in 2004 that "I decided not to do it because I didn't think it would be fair to all the artists that I want to work with. I'm really hard on myself when it comes to my own record, so it would have taken nine or ten months of my time. I could get two or three artists' albums done in that amount of time, so I decided just to back off of it. I cut a couple of songs, and I was digging the way I was sounding on the mic. There's always something to write about. I mean if I didn't have a label to run, and a lot of artists to put out, it would be a different story, then I could just totally concentrate on self. Building my company and getting these artists out is my main priority right now. I spread out the tracks that I did for the record to the other artists I'm working with. I don't think anybody's going to be mad about it after they hear what I'm doing."

Dre eventually backed off both of the aforementioned excuses, and returned to work on his greatest masterpiece yet, apparently rediscovering his relevance to the game on a personal level, explaining more recently that "I don't think it's a young man's game. It's all in how you're putting it together, and how you're carrying yourself. If you feel old, it's going to turn out like that. I don't even think about that. I feel like I could turn 50 and still make a hot hip-hop record...I don't I want to necessarily see a 50-year old rapper, but being behind the scenes, making tracks, and producing, there's no age limit on that. It's all about who's keeping it hot. You could make a hot hip-hop record if you're 70, you just gotta know what's going on in here, and know what the people want. If people are talking about somebody being too old, that means that sound is getting too old. It's time to start your game over, reinvent yourself or something."

Rediscovering himself artistically was the first step for Dre. The next was to transition back to his own album from other projects in the studio, which was quite a juggle according to producer's recording schedule as laid out by longtime collaborator Scott Storch, "Detox is in production right now...Dre wants this to surpass Chronic and for him to do that it might just take that much longer because he needs to dedicate all his energy on that but right now he's busy with Busta Rhymes and Eve and Game's next record, so he's trying to do all those things...He's got a lot going on for him to focus on one project. But I gotta tell you man the stuff I'm hearing right now 'OH MY GOD' the game will not be the same EVER. He did one beat that he said he wanted Jay Z to jump on and if that happens they can both retire for good. And not just Dre other producers are bringing their best work to the table."

Elaborating on the creative process behind the epic production sessions for 'Detox', longtime collaborator Mel Man explained that "Dre has been kicking around ideas and concepts for Detox for a long time. He changed his mind a few times and was never really happy enough about any of them. There is immense pressure to make Detox groundbreaking and better than his first two solo albums. In addition to that this is Dre's final solo album, so there is the additional pressure of going out with a bang that will echo in eternity. I don't think it ever crossed Dre's mind to actually not do Detox. Announcing that he wasn't helped relieve some of the pressure. It also allowed Dre to step back and get his mind off of it for a while and get a fresh start later on. That fresh start is now as Detox is definitely back on. That we are actually putting vocals on some tracks is a very important step. For the last few years we have been building hundreds of instrumentals for Detox. They ranged from really sparse and simple beats to some of the craziest and most complex beats you have ever heard. We have all worked very hard together to create something truly original and groundbreaking. Picking which ones to actually use is easier said than done. Dre pushes us to dig deep and put our own ideas into the skeleton instrumentals we have made alongside him for Detox over the last couple of years. We are really pushing the envelope. In my opinion Dre has thrown out some incredible tracks that we and Dre have built together, but Dre is looking for something specific and if he doesn't hear it he will not use it…At least that is the direction Dre has gone so far. I think the early tracks are as good as anything Dre has ever done—but it is still too early to tell how the final album will sound. I'm confident you will be very pleased. Dre is planning something special for the album's last track—if we can keep it within the budget…I think you will hear Detox in 5.1…Dre wants to do it himself, which means it will take him a lot of time (it takes him a month for a regular CD so imagine how long it will take for a 6 channel mix). Dre really wants to create a mind blowing musical experience for you to enjoy one day, so I have no doubt you will one day get a chance to hear Dre take this format to a whole new level...We have a long way to go but I think Dre is finally at peace with what he/we are trying to achieve on Detox. One thing to consider is this: The Vibe award incident really had a big impact on Dre. I have never seen Dre as determined and focused as he is right now. His anger and will to defeat all those who try to bring him down are having a direct impact on the aggressive nature of his recent productions. I promise you that no one is as driven as Dre is to make Detox, FUBAR the competition or anyone who stands in his way. I don't know what the outcome of Detox will be, but we all, especially Dre will work to exhaustion to make Detox the best it can be."

That whole new level, according to Scott Storch, would produce "the most advanced rap album musically and lyrically we'll probably ever have a chance to listen to."

Stepping back up to the mic to speak on his own behalf regarding the album's progress, Dre explained that conceptually, before he could continue working on the record, "I had to come up with something different but still keep it hardcore, so what I decided to do was make my album one story about one person and just do the record through a character's eyes...And everybody that appears on my album is going to be a character, so it's basically going to be a hip-hop musical... I've been blueprinting, getting ideas together for the past six months or so, just trying to figure out which direction I want to take and how I'm gonna present the project...Just gathering sounds and what have you. I want this one to be really over the top."

Focused enough by this point to look even past the completion and release of his final solo album, Dre's musical ambitions for the future were as advanced as ever, involving a mix of some of the new and some of the classics, such that, according to the producer, "hopefully, I'll...score a movie or two…I'll definitely be making hip-hop records, looking for new, hot artists. I'm really trying to score some movies though, that's what I'm working on. That's a big challenge. To conduct a big ass string section doing something that I wrote would be ridiculous. That's the dream right now."

Still, for the most part, Dre seemed to prefer to remain in the moment when thinking about the future creatively, knowing that one was the means to the other's end, explaining that "my thing is just coming in here and making records, and hopefully people will go out and buy it and bump it. I'm just trying to come in and better myself when I'm in here. If I had to give an answer (as to my legacy)…I'd say that I'd like to be remembered as a person who really cared about his music, and really entertained people with my talent."

Dre—like any artist—clearly desires to be recognized for his overall catalog in any retrospective celebration of his legacy. Still, the Dr—better than perhaps any other figure in hip hop—knows that you're only as relevant as your last hit record. In that context, Dre clearly has been seeking to construct a soundtrack of hip hop genius that will score enough hits and break enough new ground to be recognized on the periphery as ahead of its time in the moment.

More importantly, in terms of the coming generations of hip hop, Dre is also seeking to dictate the way hip hop marks musical progress for the coming future according to the standards he sets with his new album—just as he did with 'The Chronic 2001' at the turn of the millennium, and 'The Chronic' at the dawn of the 1990s. As complicated as all the aforementioned sounds, Dre keeps it simple in summarizing on how he desires to be remembered once he's finally gone from the game, "I just want to be remembered as being the shit."

As far as hip hop production will ever be concerned, he has already cemented that distinction with over 80 Million records sold. For all the records Dre has broken in the course of making records, the key to his longevity always has—and will continue to—rest in the fact that he stayed about the music, both outside and *in the studio…*

Dr. Dre Discography

N.W. A. Recordings with Dr. Dre

- ▼ *N.W.A. Legacy* 1988-98
- ▼ *N.W.A. Anniversary Tribute* 1998
- ▼ *Greatest Hits* 1996
- ▼ *Niggaz4life* 1991
- ▼ *Straight Outta Compton* 1988
- ▼ *N.W.A. & The Posse* 1987

Also, Producer for major recording artists including Snoop Dogg, Tupac Shakur and Eminem.

He has contributed to the following movie soundtracks:
- ▼ *Bullworth, Natural Born Killers, Deep Cover, Wild Wild West* and *Friday.*

Dr. Dre Solo Discography

1992

- ▼ Dre formed Death Row Records with Suge Knight after leaving N.W.A.

April

- ▼ Dre could be heard with the hit "Nuthin' But A 'G' Thang" which also introduced rapper Snoop Doggy Dogg.
- ▼ The Chronic was released.

- ▼ Dre hit the Top 40 and the Top 10 with "Nuthin' But A "G" Thang."
- ▼ Dre topped the Billboard Top R&B Singles chart for 2 weeks with "Nuthin' But A "G" Thang."
- ▼ The Chronic topped the Billboard Top R&B Albums chart for 8 weeks.
- ▼ The Chronic was certified platinum and the single "Nuthin' But A 'G' Thang" was certified platinum.
- ▼ Dre topped the Billboard Hot 100 Singles Sales chart for a week and the Hot Rap Singles chart for 3 weeks with "Nuthin' But A "G" Thang."

May

- ▼ The Chronic was certified 2x platinum.
- ▼ Dre hit the Top 40 with "Dre Day."

June

- ▼ Dre hit the Top 10 with "Dre Day."

July

- ▼ Dre topped the Billboard Hot Dance Music Maxi-Singles Sales chart for a week with "Dre Day."

August

- ▼ The single "Dre Day" was certified gold.

September

- ▼ The video for "Nuthin' But A 'G' Thang" was nominated for a MTV Video Music Award for Best Rap Video.
- ▼ Dre produced the multi-platinum debut of Snoop Doggy Dogg—Doggystyle.

October

- ▼ Dr. Dre hit the Top 40 with "Let Me Ride."

November

▼ The Chronic was certified 3x platinum.

December

▼ Dr. Dre topped the Billboard Year-End Charts as the Top New Pop Artist, Top Hot 100 Singles Artist—Male, Top R&B Artist (singles & albums), Top R&B Artist—Male (singles & albums), Top New R&B Artist, Top R&B Album Artist, Top R&B Album Artist—Male, and Top R&B Singles Artist—Male.

1994

February

▼ Dre won 2 American Music Awards for Favorite Rap/Hip-Hop Artist and Favorite New Rap/Hip-Hop Artist.

March

▼ Dre won a Grammy Award for Best Rap Solo Performance ("Let Me Ride") and was nominated for Best Rap Performance by a Duo or Group ("Nuthin' But A 'G' Thang" with Snoop Doggy Dogg).

May

▼ Dre won Source Awards for Artist of the Year (Solo), Album of the Year, and Producer of the Year.

September

▼ The video for "Let Me Ride" was nominated for a MTV Video Music Award for Best Rap Video.

October

▼ The Dre-produced compilation Concrete Roots—Anthology was released with the Dre tracks "Dre's Beat Re-mix," "The Planet," "Dre's Beat," "Must Be The Music" (World Class Wreckin' Cru), and "The Grand Finale" (N.W.A.).

1995

▼ # 73 Singles Artist of the Year

▼ Dre spent 5 months in prison for violating his parole.

▼ Dre hit the Top 40 with "Keep Their Heads Ringin'" from the Friday soundtrack.

▼ The single "Keep Their Heads Ringin'" was certified gold.

September

▼ Dre won a MTV Video Music Award for "Keep Their Heads Ringin'."

1996

▼ # 134 Singles Artist of the Year

January

▼ Dre hit the Top 40 helping out 2Pac with "California Love."

February

▼ Dre was nominated for a Grammy Award for Best Rap Solo Performance ("Keep Their Heads Ringin'").

March

- ▼ Dre hit the Top 10 helping out 2Pac with "California Love."
- ▼ A collection of Dre's early material was released—First Round Knock Out.
- ▼ Dre left Death Row Records and formed Aftermath Entertainment. The break from Death Row also began a public bitterness between Dre and Suge Knight.

September

- ▼ Dre was nominated for a MTV Video Music Award for Best Rap Video with 2Pac ("California Love").
- ▼ Dre helped out Blackstreet on a remix of their hit "No Diggity."

November

- ▼ Dre released the compilation Dr. Dre Presents...The Aftermath with the hit "Been There Done That."

1997

- ▼ # 203 Singles Artist of the Year

February

- ▼ Dre was nominated for a Grammy Award for Best Rap Performance by a Duo or Group ("California Love" with 2Pac and Roger Troutman).

September

- ▼ Dre was nominated for 4 MTV Video Music Awards for Best Rap Video ("No Diggity" with Blackstreet and "Been There Done That"), Best Choreography ("Been There Done That"), and Best R&B Video ("No Diggity" with Blackstreet).

1999

March

- Eminem hit the Top 40 with "My Name Is."

September

- Dre was nominated for a MTV Video Music Award for Best Direction for Eminem's "My Name Is."

October

- Dre appeared on Saturday Night Live with Eminem.

November

- Dr. Dre 2001 was released.

December

- Dr. Dre 2001 topped the Billboard R&B Albums chart for 3 weeks.
- MTV: 100 Greatest Videos Ever Made includes "California Love" with 2Pac at #9 and "Nuthin' But A 'G' Thang" (with Snoop Doggy Dogg) at #32.

2000

- #100 Singles Artist of the Year

January

- Dr. Dre 2001 was certified 2x platinum.

February

- Dre was nominated for 2 Grammy Awards for Rap Performance by a Duo or Group ("Still D.R.E." with Snoop Dogg and "Guilty Conscience" with Eminem).
- Dr. Dre 2001 was certified 3x platinum.

March

- ▼ Dre hit the Top 40 with help from Eminem with "Forgot About Dre."
- ▼ Dr. Dre 2001 was certified 4x platinum.
- ▼ Dre filed a lawsuit against Napster over their file-sharing program, which allowed users to download music for free. Dre had warned the company previously to have his material removed and "de-listed" or he would file a lawsuit.

May

- ▼ Eminem hit the Top 40 with "The Real Slim Shady" and the video hit #1 on MTV's Top 20 Video Countdown.
- ▼ Dre, Snoop Dogg, Eminem, MC Ren, and Ice Cube kicked off a tour together in California.
- ▼ Dr. Dre 2001 was certified 5x platinum.
- ▼ Eminem hit the Top 10 with "The Real Slim Shady" and the song's video hit #1 on the MTV Top 20 Video Countdown.
- ▼ Dre hit the Top 40 with help from Snoop Dogg on "The Next Episode."

September

- ▼ Dre won a MTV Video Music Award for Best Rap Video ("Forgot About Dre" with Eminem) and was also nominated for Best Direction for Eminem's "The Real Slim Shady."
- ▼ Eminem hit the Top 40 with "The Way I Am."

November

- ▼ Dr. Dre 2001 was certified 6x platinum.

December

▼ Dre topped the Billboard Year-End Charts with the Top R&B/Hip-Hop Album (Dr. Dre 2001) and as the Top R&B/Hip-Hop Album Artist and Top R&B/Hip-Hop Album Artist—Male.

2001

January

▼ Dre won an American Music Award for Favorite Rap/Hip-Hop Artist.

March

▼ Dre won 2 Grammy Awards for Best Rap Performance by a Duo or Group ("Forgot About Dre" with Eminem) and Producer of the Year and was nominated for Best Rap Album (Dr. Dre 2001) and Best Rap Performance by a Duo or Group ("The Next Episode" with Snoop Dogg). Dre spoke up after the awards about the controversy with Eminem's multiple nominations and performance, stating that this likely led to them losing the Album of the Year award (Eminem's The Marshall Mathers LP): "…I think we were robbed."

April

▼ Dre hit the Top 40 with Eminem with "Forgot About Dre."

▼ VH1: 100 Greatest Videos includes "Nothin' But A 'G' Thang" at # 80.

August

▼ Dre was nominated for a MTV Video Music Award for Best Direction for directing Eminem's "Stan."

About the Author

Jake Brown resides in Nashville, Tennessee. An avid writer he has penned several books, including the best-sellers: *Suge Knight – The Rise, Fall & Rise of Death Row Records*; *Your Body's Calling Me: The Life and Times of Robert "R" Kelly – Music Love, Sex & Money* and *Ready To Die: The Story of Biggie—Notorious B.I.G.*; *50 Cent: No Holds Barred; Jay-Z and the Roc-A-Fella Dynasty*; *Tupac Shakur (2-Pac) In the Studio: The Studio Years (1987-1996)* and *Kanye West In the Studio: Beats Down! Money Up! The Studio Years (2000-2006)*.

ORDER FORM

WWW.AMBERBOOKS.COM

Fax Orders: 480-283-0991
Telephone Orders: 480-460-1660
Postal Orders: Send Checks & Money Orders to:
   Amber Books
   1334 E. Chandler Blvd., Suite 5-D67, Phoenix, AZ 85048
Online Orders: E-mail: Amberbk@aol.com

_____ Kanye West in the Studio, ISBN #: 0-9767735-6-2, $16.95
_____ Tupac Shakur—(2Pac) In The Studio, ISBN#: 0-9767735-0-3, $16.95
_____ Jay-Z…and the Roc-A-Fella Dynasty, ISBN#: 0-9749779-1-8, $16.95
_____ Your Body's Calling Me: The Life & Times of "Robert" R. Kelly, ISBN#: 0-9727519-5-52, $16.95
_____ Ready to Die: Notorious B.I.G., ISBN#: 0-9749779-3-4, $16.95
_____ Suge Knight: The Rise, Fall, and Rise of Death Row Records, ISBN#: 0-9702224-7-5, $21.95
_____ 50 Cent: No Holds Barred, ISBN#: 0-9767735-2-X, $16.95
_____ Aaliyah—An R&B Princess in Words and Pictures, ISBN#: 0-9702224-3-2, $10.95
_____ You Forgot About Dre: Dr. Dre & Eminem, ISBN#: 0-9702224-9-1, $10.95
_____ Divas of the New Millenium, ISBN#: 0-9749779-6-9, $16.95
_____ Michael Jackson: The King of Pop, ISBN#: 0-9749779-0-X, $29.95
_____ The House that Jack Built (Hal Jackson Story), ISBN#: 0-9727519-4-7, $16.95

Name:_____
Company Name:_____
Address:_____
City:_____ State:_____ Zip:_____
Telephone: (____) _____ E-mail:_____

For Bulk Rates Call: **480-460-1660**   ORDER NOW

Kanye West	$16.95	☐ Check ☐ Money Order ☐ Cashiers Check
Tupac Shakur	$16.95	☐ Credit Card: ☐ MC ☐ Visa ☐ Amex ☐ Discover
Jay-Z…	$16.95	
Your Body's Calling Me:	$16.95	CC#_____
Ready to Die: Notorious B.I.G.	$16.95	Expiration Date:_____
Suge Knight:	$21.95	**Payable to:**
50 Cent: No Holds Barred,	$16.95	Amber Books
Aaliyah—An R&B Princess	$10.95	1334 E. Chandler Blvd., Suite 5-D67
Dr. Dre & Eminem	$10.95	Phoenix, AZ 85048
Divas of the New Millenium,	$16.95	
Michael Jackson: The King of Pop	$29.95	**Shipping:** $5.00 per book. Allow 7 days for delivery.
The House that Jack Built	$16.95	**Sales Tax:** Add 7.05% to books shipped to Arizona addresses.
		Total enclosed: $_____